the kids' building workshop

the kids' building workshop

15 Woodworking Projects for Kids and Parents to Build Together

J. Craig and Barbara Robertson
with their daughters Camille and Allegra

The mission of Storey Publishing is to serve our customers by publishing practical information that encourages personal independence in harmony with the environment.

Edited by Nancy W. Ringer

Cover design by Wendy Palitz & Vicky Vaughn

Text design by Wendy Palitz

Text production by Karin Stack

Cover and interior photographs by Edward Judice

Illustrations by Alison Kolesar

Indexed by Susan Olason, Indexes & Knowledge Maps

Copyright © 2004 by J. Craig and Barbara Robertson

The information in this book is true and complete to the best of our knowledge. All recommendations are made without guarantee on the part of the authors or Storey Publishing. The authors and publisher disclaim any liability in connection with the use of this information. For additional information please contact Storey Publishing, 210 MASS MoCA Way, North Adams, MA 01247.

Storey books are available for special premium and promotional uses and for customized editions. For further information, please call 1-800-793-9396.

Printed in the United States by Edward Brothers
10 9 8 7 6 5 4 3 2 1

Library of Congress Cataloging-in-Publication Data

Robertson, J. Craig.
    Kids' building workshop : 15 woodworking projects for kids and parents to build together / J. Craig and Barbara Robertson.
        p. cm.
    Includes bibliographical references and index.
    ISBN 1-58017-488-4 (pb : alk. paper) — ISBN 1-58017-572-4 (hc : alk. paper)
    1. Woodwork. 2. Woodworking tools. I. Robertson, Barbara. II. Title.
TT185.R656 2004
684'.08—dc22
                                                                        2004001521

thanks

The authors — Craig, Barbara, Camille, and Allegra — would like to thank everyone who helped out with this book. Special thanks go to our photo-shoot carpenters: Sarah, Katherine, and Melissa Brink; Lucas and Trudy Ames; Orelia and Geneva Jonathan; Gregory and Jacob Goldstone; Kelsey Shanley; Hailey Newbound; Zachary, Amalia, and Sophia Leamon; Kimberly Houston; and Benjamin and Daniel Joslyn. What a gang!

Words of gratitude are due to the members of our first building crews: Dylan and Evan Dethier (a.k.a. our first, and best, lemonade salesmen); Nancy Nylen; and Isaiah, Naomi, and Otha Day. Thanks also to John Kleiner and his two sons Matthew and Aaron for sharing their birdhouse design with us.

One last thank-you goes to Nancy Ringer, our editor, for her patience, flexibility, and calm ways.

contents

introduction 1

PART 1

setting up shop:
getting to know your tools

HAMMERING 6

SAWING 10

    Furniture Factory 16

DRILLING 20

    You Name It 24

BLOCK PLANE 26

    The Perfect Curl 28

MEASURING 30

    Checkerboard 34

PART 2

down to business: building your own projects

String Art 40

Twin Birdhouse .46

Single Birdhouse 52

Sturdy Stool 56

Cricket Cage 62

Perfect Toolbox 68

Horse Sawhorses 74

Flip It 82

Allegra's Table .92

Bookhouse 102

Lemonade Stand 114

Puppet Theater 126

index 136

iNtroductioN

Who isn't at least a little delighted by a shiny new hammer? And who doesn't feel just a little empowered by successfully drilling a clean hole through an otherwise solid board? When kids first encounter hammers, they almost instantly know what they are for. If they're lucky, nails and wood are nearby, as well as willing parents who will allow them to drive nail after nail, experimenting with various ways of pulling out the crooked ones and trying a variety of methods to keep a wiggly board still. Some parents, noting that tools can be heavy, sharp, and even a bit dangerous, don't allow their children access to carpentry tools. This well-intentioned effort to avoid blackened fingernails and Band-Aids may also mean that the children don't get to master the use of simple tools at a young age.

With this book we hope to share enough tips, give enough good advice, and create enough enthusiasm to allow parents and children to develop basic carpentry skills. We've mapped out a variety of projects — from simple to more complex — that allow families to work together to create some fun, well-designed items. Our hope? That these projects will be only the beginning! If you make the projects in this book, if you become the proud producer of everything from decorative string art and perfectly curled wood shavings to a drawing table and a lemonade stand, you should be ready to take on carpentry projects of your own design and maybe even in your own home.

We wrote this book as a family, each of us bringing our own skills and perspective to the project. Craig is a builder who has remodeled many homes, including two of our own when our daughters were young. He has more than twenty years of experience in carpentry. Barbara is the director of education at an art museum and has spent an equal number of years teaching art to children and writing curriculum and lesson plans. When we began the process of writing this book, Camille was eleven and Allegra was nine. (The "to kids" boxes scattered throughout the book are written by Camille.) They'd both been swinging hammers for many years and had plenty of opinions they were eager to share about the subject of carpentry. Having lived through many building projects together, we thought it might be fun to write a book about carpentry together, too. And it has been. We hope you'll have as much fun learning carpentry with your family.

A word about safety: There will always be some danger in working with carpentry tools, and beginners need to be made aware of potential hazards. Even if you are tackling the simplest projects in this book, make sure you are comfortable with the task you have set for yourself and your family. Read and reread the sections on tool use, take your time, and pay close attention when working with a sharp or powerful tool. Remember, the competent use of a tool will always be the safest use. We have done our best throughout the book to point out where risks lie and strategies for coping with them. But we can't put in writing every solution to every potential danger; use common sense and seek more help if you need it.

The organization: This book is organized into two basic sections. The first gives you information and tips for using the tools that will become your trusted friends and companions in carpentry. Read this section first! For each tool, we have provided safety tips and handling advice, as well as a project that will help you get started using that tool correctly.

The second section contains woodworking projects, arranged in order from the simplest to the most complex. Read through an entire project before you begin, even before you purchase your materials! Thoroughly preparing before you begin your project will save you time and money and encourage blessed family happiness. Make sure you know everything you can about the tools, materials, skills, and estimated time it will take to make a project before you begin.

We have written the directions for projects as though a child would be doing each step. But that doesn't mean that you should enforce a child-only regime. There will be times when an adult will want to take over, especially for some of the more challenging measuring and cutting and the more repetitive tasks. Work together and choose the most appropriate person on your team to do each job. Over time, you may find that the children's skills outpace the parents'! Approach each project with an eye for maximizing family fun. Save the best jobs for the kids, and let them experiment and make some mistakes, too.

Must-have tools

These are the tools we think you really need — not only to make the projects in this book, but also to take on projects of your own design. Buying tools is fun, and browsing in a good hardware store or lumberyard is a treat. But you don't need half of what's out there. Start with the basics, and expand your collection over time and as your expertise grows.

FOR KIDS
Handsaw
Block plane
Drill
Hammer (16 ounces)
Measuring tape
Clamps
Screwdrivers (Phillips and slotted)
Compass
Speed Square
Combination square
Ruler
Awl
Nail set
Nail apron
Safety glasses

FOR ADULTS
Circular saw
Jigsaw
Cordless drill
Utility knife
Staple gun
Ear protection (headphones or ear plugs) for use with power tools
Safety glasses

part

1

setting up shop:

getting to know your tools

Hammering

THE BASICS

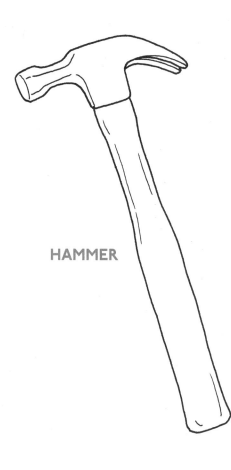

HAMMER

NAIL SET

Driving a nail through two pieces of wood to fasten them together is probably the most basic task in carpentry. And the hammer itself is probably the most basic carpenter's tool. Not only does your hammer help you drive nail after nail, but it also doubles as a pry bar, a digging tool, a hatchet, or a handy extension of your own arm.

The first key to hammering is momentum. The gathering force you can create by the swing of your arm, elbow, wrist, and hand is what powers the blow of your hammer. Imagine that you are swinging a weight at the end of a string. While you could grab the weight in your hand and hit an object directly with it, the blow will be much stronger if you can line up all the forces required to swing it in an arc.

The farther your grip is from the hammer head, the more force you will be able to get from each blow. You should grip the hammer as far from its head as you can manage while still controlling the swing.

The second key to hammering success is to *hit hard!*

Much of the force of a hammer strike goes into convincing the nail to overcome its own inertia and the substantial resistance of the wood fibers. If it takes 50 pounds of force to drive a nail into a piece of pine, then all the 45-pound blows in the world will not make that nail budge. It is not hard to imagine that a 70-pound blow will be far more effective than a half dozen 52-pound blows!

This principle also applies when you're starting a nail. Many people swing cautiously, worried perhaps about hitting their fingers instead of the nail. The result is a multitude of ineffective taps and a greater number of chances to hit those fingers. When it comes to hammering, hold the nail firmly, aim carefully, and swing like you mean it. The nail will know that you mean business!

Raise your hammer high,

swing like you mean it, and

drive the nail home.

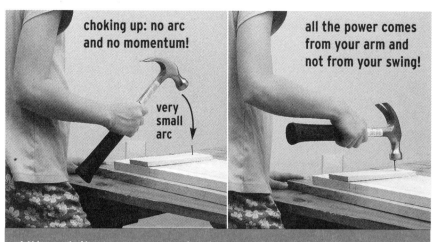

choking up: no arc and no momentum!

very small arc

all the power comes from your arm and not from your swing!

Although it may seem easier to use a hammer when you hold it close to its head, you lose momentum and you can't swing hard — breaking the two principles of successful hammering!

When Hammering Goes Wrong

There are, of course, a few things that typically go wrong. Bending a nail is the result of a hammer swing that does not align properly with the shank of the nail. To avoid bending a nail, take a good look at where the nail is pointing and try to make your swing come down as if it intended to pass through the head of the nail and down the shank all the way to the point. If you do bend a nail, you can straighten it using the claw of the hammer and then drive it again, but it is likely to bend again. Usually it's best to pull out the bent nail and start a fresh nail in the same hole.

Another frequent hammering mishap is the crooked or misdirected nail. If your nail does not go where you want it to, pull it out and start again. But don't put your nail back in the same hole! This will simply tell your nail that you want it to take the same misguided path. Instead, start the nail in a new spot.

And finally, pulling out a nail is a trick all of its own. You can use your hammer claw for this. Slip the claw under the head of the nail so that the nail shank rests in the **V** of the claw. Insert a block of wood under the hammer head; the block will give you better leverage for pulling the nail and protect your workpiece from damage. Hold the board down firmly, grip near the end of the hammer handle, and pull the handle back toward you.

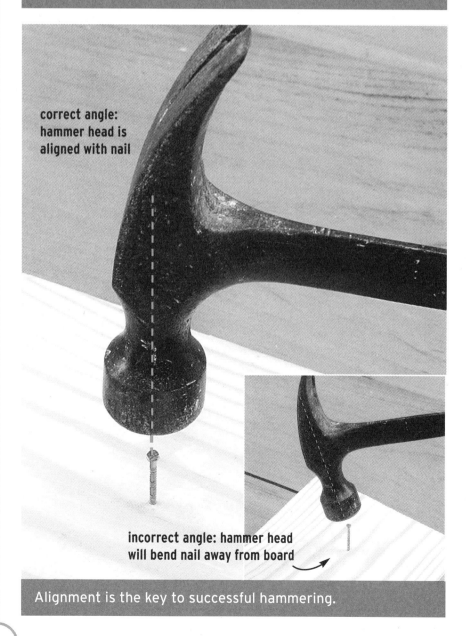

correct angle: hammer head is aligned with nail

incorrect angle: hammer head will bend nail away from board

Alignment is the key to successful hammering.

Use a block of wood for leverage when you're pulling a nail. It also will protect the surface of your workpiece.

Camille says: "Hammering is one of my favorite parts of carpentry. When I was younger, I would visit my dad's construction sites and hammer nails into scrap wood for hours. Hammering is something almost every project has. You should try to get good at hammering right at the beginning; that way, when you get to the hammering parts you'll enjoy them!"

kids!

Don't feel bad if you have to pull out a nail from time to time. Look carefully at the tool in your hand and you'll see that it was made just as much to remove nails as to drive them in!

Using a Nail Set

Certain projects demand a finished surface — one that is not interrupted by a pattern of nail heads. The best way to achieve this is with a nail set, a simple little tool that helps you set a nail head flush with, or below, the surface of a board. Setting a nail also ensures that the head of the nail is pulled tight against the wood, which maximizes its holding power.

To use a nail set, grasp its body with your free hand. Set the tip on the head of the nail you wish to sink and align the body with the shaft of the nail (this can be a little tricky and involves

guesswork at times). Hold the nail set tightly, aim carefully, and hit the top of the tool firmly with your hammer. Check the result, reposition the nail set, and hit it again. Continue until the nail head is sunk just below the surface of the board.

Keep a tight grip on the nail set, and keep it aligned with the shaft of the nail.

Sawing

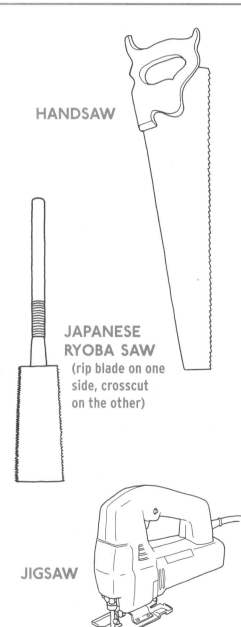

HANDSAW

JAPANESE
RYOBA SAW
(rip blade on one
side, crosscut
on the other)

JIGSAW

Cutting a piece of wood to make it fit just right is the essence of carpentry. It's fun, sometimes frustrating, and occasionally hazardous. There are many types of saws, and each must be handled in a particular way to accomplish the task for which it is most appropriate. In most instances, a handsaw will do the trick. But there are occasions when a power tool is really the only practical choice.

Choosing a Handsaw

Sawing involves two strokes: a push stroke and a pull stroke. The teeth on most saws are designed to cut on only one of these strokes. Most Americans are familiar with saws that cut on the push stroke, but the Japanese long ago developed saws that cut on the pull stroke. Pull saws are less likely to buckle during sawing and can have a blade that is much thinner than that of Western-style push saws. Some American toolmakers have begun manufacturing pull saws (such as the Shark Saw). Many of

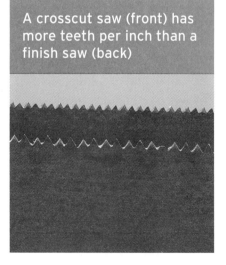

The kerf is the groove cut into the wood by the teeth of the saw.

A crosscut saw (front) has more teeth per inch than a finish saw (back)

the kids who built projects with us found working with a pull saw much easier and more satisfying than working with a traditional push saw.

If you turn a saw upside down and sight down the row of teeth, you'll notice that the tips of the teeth curl outward. This is called the set of the teeth, and it allows the saw to cut a kerf (groove) into the wood that is wider than the main body of the saw blade. When you use the saw to make a cut, the set of the teeth determines the width of the kerf. If you compare two saws, you may also notice that one has more teeth per inch (t.p.i.) than the other. A saw with fewer teeth and a more pronounced set will make a wider kerf, cut faster, and leave a rougher edge behind. A finish saw will have more teeth per inch and a narrower set. It will make a smaller kerf, cut more slowly, and leave a smoother edge behind.

For kids, the best balance is a saw with small teeth and plenty of set. With small teeth, each one will take a smaller bite into the wood. The greater set provides a wider kerf, which will mean less of a chance that the saw will bind (catch in the wood or rub against the sides of the cut).

Some new, shorter saws are manufactured without any set to the teeth at all. These saws bind very easily and should be avoided. A good first saw is a crosscut saw 15 to 20 inches long with nine to twelve teeth (or points, as they are sometimes called) per inch.

Keep your eyes on your saw cut!

Stand almost perpendicular to the cut you are going to make and clamp or hold your board securely.

Using a Handsaw

The key to making any handsaw work is alignment. Properly lined up, a saw will glide through the kerf it has made in a piece of wood with only the cutting teeth resisting the carpenter's push. If the saw starts to bind against the sides of the cut, it will become harder to push and may become impossible to move altogether! The extra exertion of using a saw that keeps binding will tire you out, and the extra pressure you'll have to use will make the saw blade more likely to pop out of the cut, which can be dangerous. So keep focused on your alignment!

To properly use your saw, start by positioning your body: Assuming you are right-handed, stand with your left foot in front of your right foot, almost perpendicular to the board you're going to cut. Your right arm should be able to move freely back and

to parents

Our kids and their friends used a range of handsaws while working on the projects in this book. They were all a little awkward at first. We've found that younger kids aren't always strong enough for sawing, nor are their arms always long enough to control the saw. Using shorter saws helps, but of course they cut more slowly. It's important to remember that everyone needs time and plenty of practice to gain confidence (and competence) with a new tool, especially a saw.

Remember too that a lot of sawing in one day is bound to tire out young carpenters. Don't feel bad if you have to revert to some adult power-sawing. We certainly do this sometimes, either ahead of time or while the kids are taking cookie breaks. Practice will make perfect, but exhaustion and exasperation will just make everyone miserable!

to parents

Sarah, one of our workshop participants, had never used a handsaw before and was getting a little frustrated. Craig came up with a little phrase that really helped. "Make it say 'Sashoom . . . sashoom,'" he said, explaining that the first syllable stood for the short, light pull stroke and the drawn-out "shooom" was the long, powerful cutting stroke. Somehow it was easier for Sarah to get the saw to make the right sound than it had been to push it through the wood. Soon her saw began to glide through the board. Encourage your kids to keep the rhythm of this phrase in their head as they saw. It might work magic for them, too!

forth across your body. You'll use your left hand to steady the board you're cutting, keeping your fingers well away from the cut. If you're left-handed, stand the opposite way, with your right foot in front of your left and your right hand steadying the board.

As you push and pull the saw to make the cut, your shoulder, elbow, wrist, and saw should be lined up. A long, even stroke is best. You might want to try a few warm-up strokes for practice, making the saw travel in a perfectly straight line in the air above your board before adding the complication of dragging it along the board's surface.

A carpenter will start a cut by setting the saw teeth on the wood, resting his thumbnail against the blade, and dragging the saw care-

fully in the opposite direction of the saw's cutting motion (toward himself for a push saw or away from himself for a pull saw). The thumb remains on the board as a guide for the first couple of strokes, until a groove has formed in the wood.

Because this method leaves fingers in harm's way, we came up with a safer method for family woodworking. We often clamp a piece of scrap wood against the line that we want to cut. Then we draw the blade against this guide until the blade has cut a deep groove in the wood. In fact, the guide block can be left in place for the entire cut. It keeps the saw blade properly aligned until the job is done, helps prevent crooked cuts, and boosts young carpenters' satisfaction in their work.

Smooth Sawing

To lessen the chance of your saw blade binding, try waxing the blade. Butcher's paste wax is the carpenter's standby, but we've used car wax and even a candle stub. The wax helps the blade glide more smoothly through the wood. Keeping your blade clean and rust-free will also improve its quality.

scrap-wood guide

Aligning the saw blade against a scrap-wood guide makes it easier to stay on course for a straight cut.

Using a Jigsaw

The jigsaw is the most practical type of saw to use to cut along a curved line (like the outline of an animal shape or a wave). Our kids were leery of using the jigsaw at first, but they quickly got the hang of it. They were really proud of themselves when they felt they'd mastered it. Always draw the cutting line first so that you are not trying to design while you cut; full attention to cutting will be needed!

The front of the plate at the bottom of a jigsaw — called the soleplate — resembles a sewing machine foot. The blade runs up and down through the plate. When you are ready to cut, rest the front of the soleplate on the board with the blade not yet making contact with the wood. Pull the trigger to start the saw, and when it is running smoothly, ease it into the cut.

The saw should cut through the wood readily; you should not have to apply much pressure for the saw to make steady progress. Keeping the soleplate flat against the wood, steer slowly and carefully, guiding the saw blade along the line you've marked.

If you have drawn a line that curves too sharply for the saw blade to follow, try backing it up just a bit and cutting along the inside edge of the kerf. By widening the kerf in this way, you give the blade more space to pivot. You may have to repeat the process several times to complete the cut. Do not try to force the blade through a sharp turn; twisting the blade will not help it make the turn and may snap the blade off.

Finally, remember to wear safety glasses while operating the jigsaw, as you should when using any power tool.

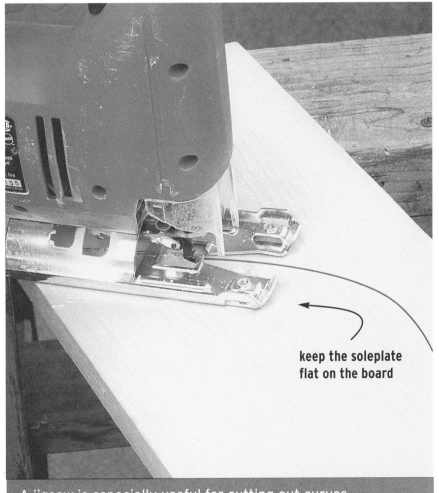

keep the soleplate
flat on the board

A jigsaw is especially useful for cutting out curves.

to parents

The jigsaw is a relatively safe tool for kids to use provided they keep both hands on the handle grip for control and always clamp down the workpiece while cutting.

Remind your kids not to start the saw while the blade is in contact with the wood. Watch out for an inexperienced user exerting sideways pressure or trying to push the saw through the cut. Help your child focus on letting the saw do the work and steering slowly and carefully along the pencil lines. Look over the proposed cut before sawing actually begins. If the design is a bit too ambitious, you may want to modify the line. Simplicity is a wonderful thing!

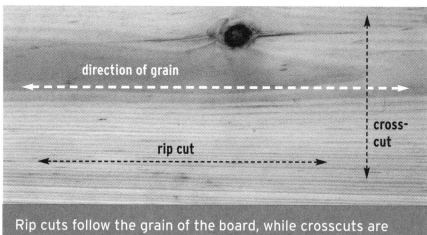

direction of grain

cross-cut

rip cut

Rip cuts follow the grain of the board, while crosscuts are made across the grain of the board.

Making Angled and Bevel Cuts

Most of the projects in this book call for making *square cuts*, or cutting straight across the board at a 90-degree angle to its top face and perpendicular to its sides. We use the term *angled cut* to designate a cut made at a 90-degree angle to the top face of the board but at another angle (say, 45 degrees) to its sides. A *bevel cut* is a cut made at any angle other than 90 degrees to the face of the board. When you are laying out a bevel cut, the angle will be drawn on the edge of the board. A cut that simultaneously angles across the face of a board and bevels the board along the cutting line is called a *compound angle cut*.

Making an angled cut with a handsaw or jigsaw is not much different from making a square cut. If you're using a handsaw, you can even clamp a scrap-wood

Ripping versus Crosscutting

Every carpenter should be familiar with the terms *rip* and *crosscut*. To crosscut means to make a cut across the grain (the direction of the wood fibers) of a piece of wood. Since the grain almost always runs the length of a board, this cut is usually made across the width of the piece. The term *crosscut* is also used to describe cutting across the width of a sheet of plywood or other material that may not have a consistent grain direction.

To rip means to cut in the same direction as the grain of a piece of wood. Ripping a board usually means cutting it along its length. This cutting operation is frequently performed on a table saw, which will rip a board to any width consistently and quickly.

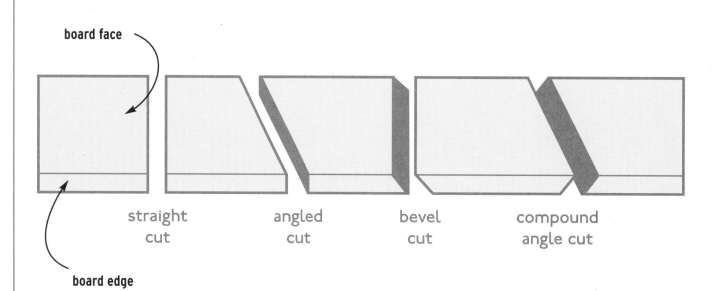

board face

straight cut

angled cut

bevel cut

compound angle cut

board edge

Allegra makes a bevel cut using the lines she's drawn on the board as guides for the blade of her Japanese ryoba saw.

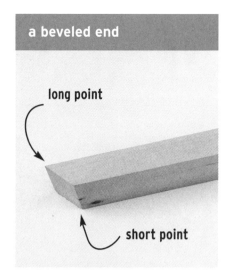

long point

short point

guide at the correct angle to help you stay on course.

Using a handsaw to make a bevel cut can be tricky. The first step is to lay out the cut on all sides of the board. Use your Speed Square to draw a line at the correct angle on both edges of the board and to square a line connecting them across the top and bottom of the board. Start the cut at the corner away from you, and keep the saw blade following the lines along the edge and the face of the board as you cut. Try to get a feel for how to position your body in order to cut along the marked angle, and hold that position steady as you cut. Check your progress along the underside of the board from time to time, making sure that the cut is not veering off the layout line. If it is, back up your saw and reroute it.

You can use a jigsaw to make a bevel cut by setting the blade to cut at any angle (follow the manufacturer's instructions to adjust the base to the correct angle). Be sure to unplug the tool before making the blade adjustment! Then position yourself so that the angle of the jigsaw blade matches the angle you've marked across the edge of the board and cut straight across the board, following the line you've drawn across the face.

When you've finished making a bevel cut, the board will end at an angle, with a long point (the edge of the face that extends farther out) and a short point (the edge of the face that is cut shorter). When the project instructions call for you to make a measurement from the beveled end of a board, they will specify which of these points to use. Many a workpiece has been miscut because of a measurement made from the wrong point of the bevel or because a bevel has its angle headed in the wrong direction. Checking twice before cutting — always a good idea in carpentry — is especially important when working with bevels.

furniture factory

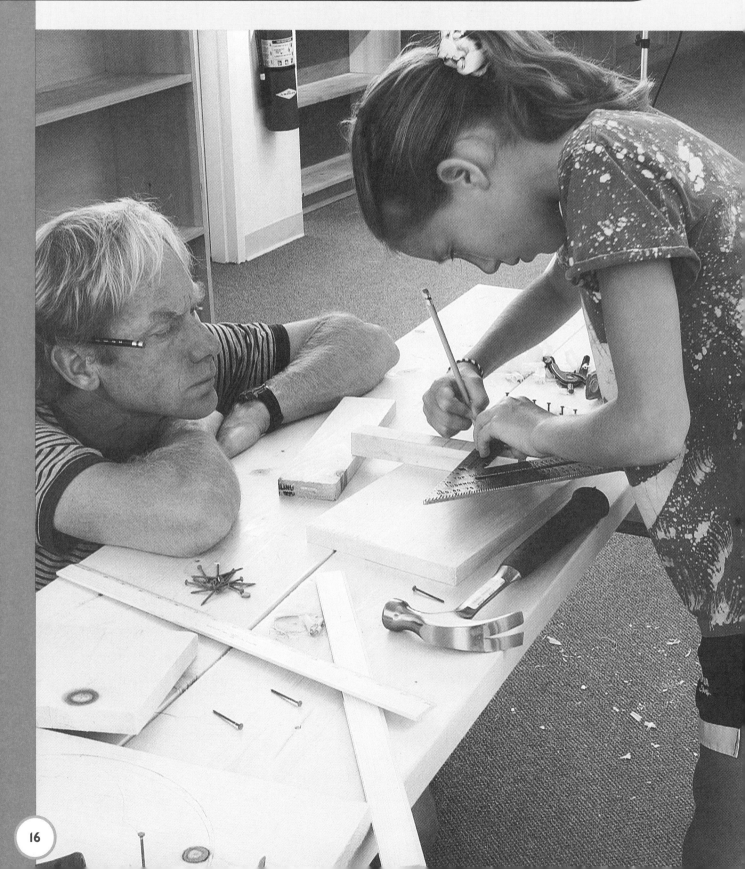

The name says it all. Your goal: to become a human furniture factory! And while you're at it, to get plenty of practice sawing and nailing. Allegra and Camille came up with the idea for this project one summer on Martha's Vineyard. They spent hours with hammers and nails turning construction-site scrap wood into pint-sized furniture for themselves and their stuffed animals.

What You'll Need

TOOLS

Clamps

Pencil

Straightedge (ruler, combination square, or Speed Square)

A variety of handsaws

Hammer

MATERIALS

A variety of boards in lengths between 20 inches and 40 inches

Scrap wood to use as a saw guide

FASTENERS

Nails (any type)

Saw, Saw, Saw

1. Clamp a board to your work surface. Using your pencil and straightedge, square a line 6 to 10 inches from one end.

2. Clamp a piece of scrap wood right up against the line you just marked to make a guide for your cut.

3. Saw through the line you've marked, keeping the saw blade straight against the guide. Make the longest stroke you can. The longer each stroke, the fewer it will take to finish your cut.

4. When you are done with a cut, grab another board (or make a new line farther down on the same board), reposition the clamps and guide, and make another cut.

to parents

A good game for kids who are learning to saw is to keep track of how many strokes it takes to cut through each board. Does the number of strokes decrease with each cut? If so, their technique is improving! A little friendly competition might be in order: Jot down the number of strokes it takes each kid to cut through a given board. The "winner" is the one with the lowest stroke score.

5. Continue marking, clamping, and sawing until you have a good supply of pieces. They should be of all different sizes. You can even use a Speed Square to mark angled cuts, giving you triangles and other odd shapes.

1

scrap wood

cutting line

2

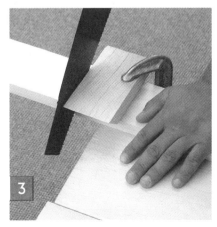

3

Hammer, Hammer, Hammer

6. Gather together your multi-sized, multi-shaped blocks of wood. Look them over; size them up. Then begin fitting them together in various combinations to make furniture. If you have a favorite stuffed animal, doll, or even small pet, you might want to build a bed or chair especially for him or her.

7. When you're happy with a particular furniture design, grab your hammer, nails, and clamps and go to work fastening it together. This stage makes for good practice in both hammering and clamping. If you can't figure out a good way to clamp a piece of furniture together so that you can drive nails into it, ask a grown-up for help.

Camille says: "I used to choke up on the hammer and swing as hard as I could, and I thought hammering was a big pain. My dad would say, 'Let the hammer do the work.' Finally I caught on to just letting the hammer drop, so that it does the driving without me using physical strength. Now I love hammering!"

kids!

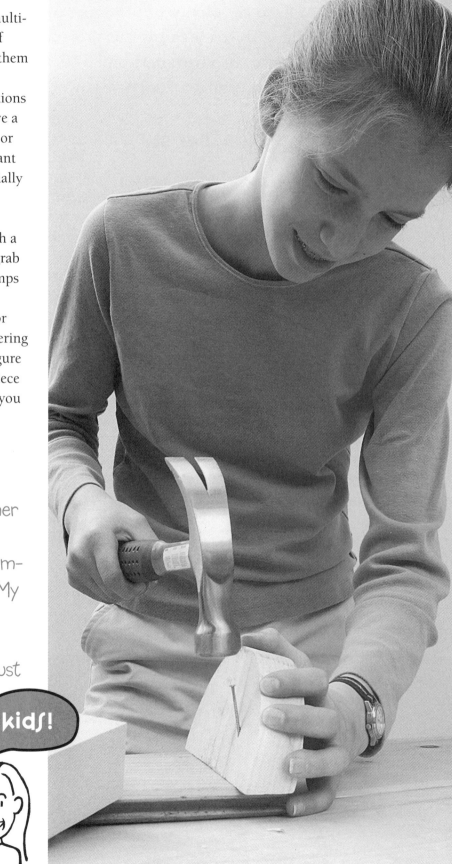

comfy chaise

barnyard bench

monkey business desk

horse house

animal armchair

drilling

THE BASICS

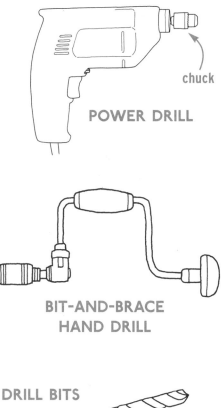

chuck

POWER DRILL

BIT-AND-BRACE HAND DRILL

DRILL BITS

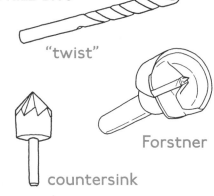

"twist"

Forstner

countersink

Basically, drilling is making a hole by pressing something hard against a surface and spinning it around and around until it bores right through. While the concept might be basic, there are a few things you should keep in mind before you go turning everything in sight into Swiss cheese.

Bits and Tidbits

There are as many kinds of drill bits as there are kinds of holes that need to be drilled. The projects in this book, however, require only "twist" bits, Forstner bits, and countersink bits.

"Twist" bits are what you probably think of as ordinary drill bits. They are used for most projects in this book, and the size required is always noted.

Forstner bits make holes with smooth sides and bottoms. You can use paddle bits, which cost less, instead, but they tend to bind and jam and make a rougher hole. We vote for using the Forstners despite the added expense.

The countersink bit makes a hole with a tapered recess at the top. The recess is necessary when you are predrilling for a screw that you want to be flush with (not protruding from) the surface of the wood.

You might encounter Fuller bits at your lumber supply store. These bits have a tapered shaft. They make a hole that matches a particular size of wood screw and also countersinks the screw in one operation. Since we use drywall screws for projects in this book, Fuller bits aren't necessary.

A countersunk hole (left) holds the screw flush with the wood surface (right).

Your foot makes a great clamp. But don't forget to put scrap wood underneath the board you're drilling!

Kids can safely use several kinds of hand drills. With training and supervision, they can use power and cordless drills as well.

Making Your Mark

The best way to mark the spot where you're going to drill a hole is *not* with a pencil dot. If you mark drilling holes ahead of time, a pencil dot can be hard to find later, and it doesn't mark the drilling spot with accuracy. Instead, draw crosshairs — two small perpendicular lines whose intersection marks the exact spot where you'll drill.

Drilling Mechanics

For basic drilling — and that is what this book calls for — holding the drill as straight as possible is crucial. If you're drilling straight down into a piece of wood, keep the bit aligned vertically. If you're drilling from the side, keep the bit aligned horizontally.

As you're drilling, apply steady pressure to keep the bit going forward into the wood. If you're right-handed, use your right hand to rotate the handgrip on a brace drill or to pull the trigger on a power drill, and use your left hand to push. If you're left-handed, do the opposite. You can use your body weight to help you push by leaning into the drill. Just be sure not to push the drill away from that vertical or horizontal alignment!

Most important, keep your eyes focused (through safety glasses, of course) on the work at hand at all times.

Keeping It Clean

When you're using a power drill, sometimes the bit will get clogged and will stop progressing through the wood. If this happens, withdraw it from the hole, with the drill still running, to clear the sawdust from the hole and the bit. If the sawdust doesn't fall away as you pull the bit out of the hole, wait until the drill stops turning and then clear the packed sawdust from the channel in the bit using the tip of a screw or nail. Be careful: The bit may be very hot!

When you're using a Forstner bit, run the drill at a slow speed so that it will cut through the wood efficiently. The proper speed will make nice helical shavings pile up around the deepening hole. Drilling too fast will just scrub the cutting edge around the bottom of the hole and heat up and dull the bit.

Camille says: "Before I had used a drill, I always kept my distance when my dad was using one. So when my dad told me I should use the drill for one of the projects in this book, I wasn't so sure it was a good idea. But my dad unplugged the drill and showed me how to use it. Then he plugged it in again, showed me where to drill the hole, and told me to try it.

"I pulled the trigger and started pushing as straight as I could. The drill was vibrating and it felt weird. But I did it!

"When I have to drill through harder pieces of wood, I have to get my mom or dad to help me, because I'm not strong enough to push the drill through by myself."

Using a Brace and Bit

One of the oldest types of hand-powered drills is the brace. You use a brace with a self-feeding bit that has a pointed screw at its tip. As you turn the brace handle, the screw turns, driving the cutting edge of the bit into the wood.

To use a brace, put your weaker hand on the big round top handle and push down while rotating the handgrip with your other hand. You can exert more force with your upper hand by leaning against it with your chest. (Some early braces were actually designed with two handgrips and a flat surface for your chest to push against.) Keep steady pressure against the brace, or the screw will strip out (pull out of the wood, taking with it the wood fibers needed to hold it in place).

A brace is a perfect tool for two kids to work together, one holding and guiding and the other cranking the brace around with both hands. Its slow turning speed makes it one of the safer cutting tools, and its powerful leverage makes it a good choice for turning large Forstner bits. Although it's not intended for them, a brace chuck usually will hold ordinary drill bits, so you can use this tool for many drilling tasks.

Using a Power Drill

Once you have the basic drilling mechanics down, using a power drill is relatively easy, as long as you are cautious. Hold the body

The brace is more fun to use when you work with a friend (or, as in this case, a brother)!

of the drill with your weaker hand and pull the trigger with your stronger. As is the case with all power tools, kids using a power drill should be supervised.

There are two basic risks in using a power drill: One is accidentally making a hole where a hole doesn't belong, such as in a tabletop, the porch floor, or someone's finger. The other, more serious risk is for a sleeve or a lock of hair to get wound around the bit or chuck. Remember, even at a relatively slow speed a power drill is turning at hundreds of revolutions per minute! So the first rule of using a power drill is **No loose ends.** If you have long hair, wear it up; if you have long sleeves, make sure they're not floppy at the ends.

A related risk is having the drill bit bind up and stop turning. Suddenly the drill itself will be doing all of the turning, which can twist your wrist around quite forcefully. Thus the second rule: **Always keep a firm grip on the drill.** In most circumstances you should have one hand on the handgrip of the drill and the other steadying the body. Keep in mind that a larger-diameter bit is more likely to bind up than a smaller one, and a paddle bit is more likely to give your wrist a yank than a Forstner bit.

A drill bit that binds can make the board you are drilling suddenly swing into motion. To prevent this, you should always follow rule three: **Clamp your workpiece tightly.**

Drill bits are specially hardened so they can keep a sharp edge. As a result, they are more brittle than other types of steel, and when they are bent they can snap into sharp, flying pieces. The first time our kids worked with a power drill, they flexed the bits and nearly broke them. And this leads to rule four: **Wear eye protection whenever you are using a power drill.**

And the final rule: **Unplug all power tools whenever they are not in use.** This means that after you are done making a hole, out comes the plug. It also means that whenever you are changing a bit, the drill must be unplugged!

Predrilling (Make Way for the Screw!)

In today's world a screw gun, or a drill with a driver bit, is often used for driving screws, which makes predrilling unnecessary. However, we strongly recommend that all carpenters learn to drive screws by hand! It is a basic skill that should be mastered, and it is an independent endeavor that does not require adult supervision. However, driving a screw through two pieces of wood using a screwdriver is hard work. Doing so without first predrilling a hole for the screw to travel through will often lead to broken or misdirected screws and a disappointing finish to your job. So in almost every instance in this book that calls for using screws, we have also called for predrilling.

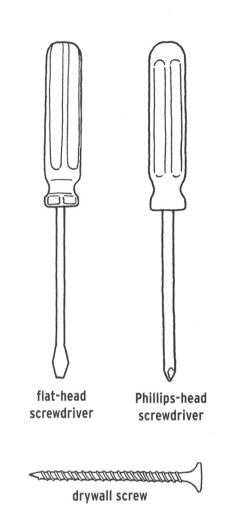

flat-head screwdriver

Phillips-head screwdriver

drywall screw

to parents

We have specified drywall screws for our projects because they are readily available and have wide threads with good gripping power. Even more important, they have a consistent shaft diameter that makes it possible for a bit that matches that diameter to be used to predrill a hole for a screw of any length. A traditional wood screw has a shank that grows thicker (and hence stronger) as it gets closer to its head. To predrill for this type of screw, you would have to use a combination of bits or a Fuller bit. For the purposes of this book, the drywall screw is a simpler, more practical solution.

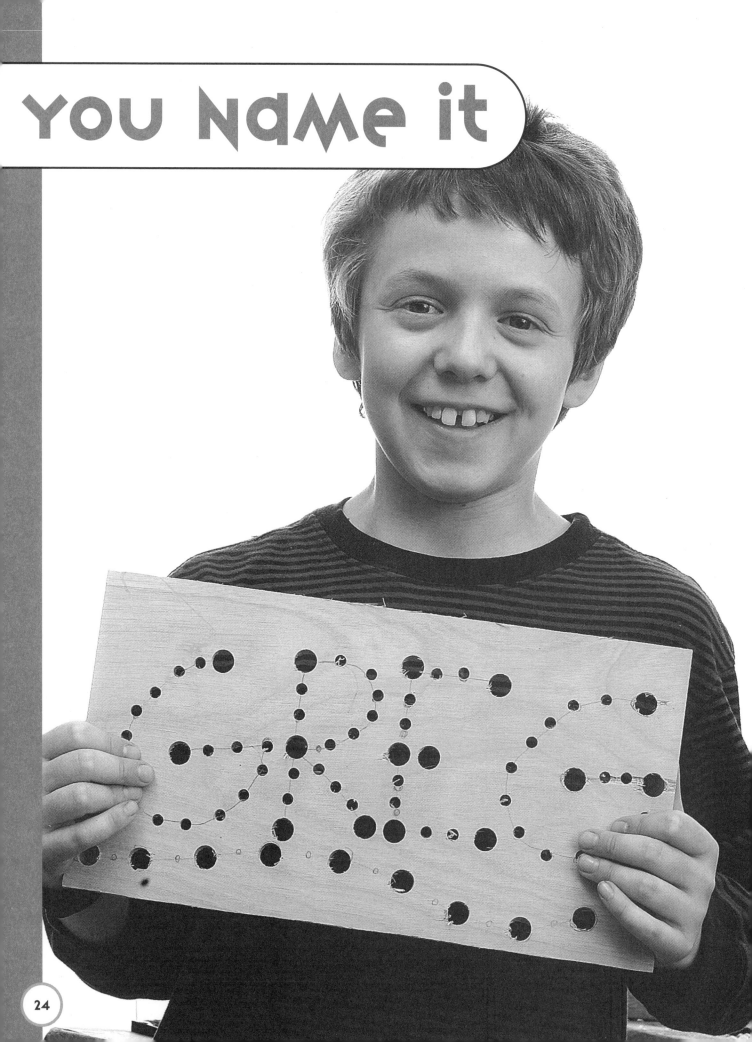

Here's a skill builder that will provide plenty of drilling practice. Not only that, you'll end up with your name in lights (sunlight, that is). Set up two or more drills (of a variety of types, if you have them) with the different bits; this way, instead of spending your time changing bits, you can just switch tools whenever you want to make a different-size hole.

What You'll Need

TOOLS

Electric or cordless drill(s)

⅛-inch drill bit

¼-inch drill bit

½-inch drill bit

Pencil

Clamps

Safety glasses

MATERIALS

A small piece of ¼-inch luaun or birch plywood

Scrap wood (plank or plywood)

Ribbon, rope, or braided yarn

Playing the Name Game

1. With a pencil, write your name on your plywood board. Block letters will make for the most straightforward work, but if you want a greater challenge, try some fancy cursive.

2. Make marks along your name where you will drill holes. If you want the holes to be evenly spaced, use a measuring tool to mark drilling spots at regular intervals. Take a look at your marks to determine if they are too close or far away from each other. Remember, taken together the marks should be readable as your name!

3. Place a piece of scrap wood under your name board and clamp both pieces securely to your work surface.

4. Put on your protective eyewear and get to work drilling holes at all the marks you have drawn. Use the same bit for all of them or mix up your bit sizes. Just be sure to drill each hole straight and all the way through your board.

Let the Light Shine Through

5. To make a handy hanging mechanism, drill a hole in each upper corner of the board. Push a length of ribbon, rope, or braided yarn through the holes and tie the ends together to form a loop.

6. Hang your name board in a window. When the sun's out, the light will shine through the letters of your name.

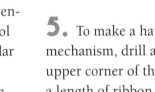

to parents

Making holes perfectly — or close to perfectly — perpendicular is one of the hard parts of drilling. Frequently remind your young drillers to keep their eyes on their work and to drill straight down into the board.

block plane

BLOCK PLANE

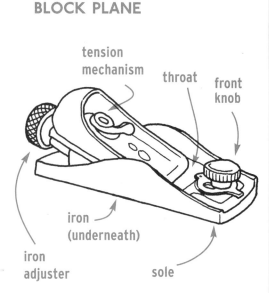

tension mechanism

throat

front knob

iron (underneath)

iron adjuster

sole

to parents

One of the simplest and most satisfying tools for a child to use, a block plane is also one of the safest. Although it should be sharp to work well, the cutting surface extends less than a sixteenth of an inch below the sole. On construction sites, the block plane has been known to remove the skin from a knuckle on occasion, but rarely more than that.

When Allegra was four years old, we did a carpentry demonstration at her preschool. After a bit of talking, all the kids got down to the real business of pushing a bronze block plane along a clear pine board. Long white curls of wood soon covered the floor: the perfect creative mess. Only the arrival of lunchtime persuaded the kids to stop working, and they all wanted a shaving to take home.

But it's not just four-year-olds who love the block plane. We used a plane at some point for every one of the projects in this book — to smooth an edge, to shorten a board that was just a little too long, or to remove an unsightly surface. Craig and his building crew keep their planes handy at all times, using them (and sharpening them) frequently. Be sure to keep your block plane close by whenever you're building!

An experienced carpenter using a sharp block plane can fit a joint so tightly that a piece of paper cannot be slipped into it. For aspiring school-age carpenters, a plane will be useful for smoothing a sawed edge or making a chamfer (bevel) on the edge of a board to give it a finished look.

Proper Planing

Proper planing technique begins with securing the workpiece by clamping it down or by setting one end against a *stop* (a fixed block that prevents the board from sliding). If you're right-handed, place your left hand on the knob at the front of the plane; this hand will guide the stroke of the plane. Wrap your right hand around the body of the plane; this hand will provide the push. If you're left-handed, set up the opposite way: right hand on the knob, left hand on the body.

Bring your body close to your workpiece, bending your elbows and tucking them in close to your sides. Position the front end

Camille planes with good form, starting at the edge of the board (left), leaning into the stroke (middle), and continuing the stroke past the end of the board (right).

of the plane sole on the near end of the board, where you want to begin planing. Then push forward, leaning a bit into the stroke and extending your arms in front of you as you plane. Most of your effort will go into making the iron slice through the wood. Just a little downward pressure (and a sharp edge) is needed to keep the tool from skipping free from the edge of the board.

The more of your body you can put into the stroke, the better. Be sure to lean forward from the waist and extend both arms as you complete the stroke. Keep an eye on the shaving as it makes its curly exit through the frog of the plane. The shaving should maintain a consistent thickness and width.

Making Adjustments

Sometimes you will need to adjust the plane to make a cut of a different depth. In almost all cases, the setting that produces the thinnest continuous shaving will be the best. Different planes may have different mechanisms for adjusting the depth of cut; many use some type of screw-driven mechanism. The following directions for making adjustments will apply to most block planes:

To adjust the iron, loosen the tension mechanism on the handle of the plane. Turn the plane upside down and sight along the sole into the light. The iron will appear as a thin shadow just above the surface of the sole. Push on the back of the iron to move it until the shadow is equally thin at all points above the sole. Tighten the tension mechanism. The tension of the screw may push the iron farther out, changing the adjustment. Test the plane and, if necessary, redo the adjustment, trying to anticipate the change that tightening the tension screw will make.

After making an adjustment, try the plane on a scrap of wood. You may find you have to adjust it again. When you like the way it cuts, the adjustment is right!

When adjusting the iron, turn the plane upside down and sight along the sole to check the iron setting.

the perfect curl

roll-up

ribbon candy

corkscrew

Camille and Allegra made up names for their curl creations.

This "project" is actually just a challenge: How long and perfect a shaving can you make with a block plane? All you need is a plane and a nice clear piece of wood. But since controlling the board while pushing the plane along one edge can be a challenge (particularly for a young carpenter), consider building the quick support we've described here. You might be surprised by what you can make, and by how much fun you'll have learning to handle your block plane.

What You'll Need

TOOLS
Block plane

Handsaw

Hammer

Clamps

MATERIALS
One 2-foot length of 1x4 or 1x6 (as free of knots as possible)

Needle and white thread (optional)

FASTENERS
Three nails

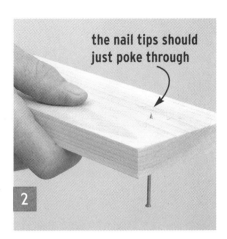

the nail tips should just poke through

2

4

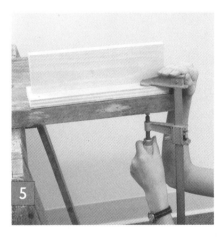

5

To Make the Support

1. Using the handsaw, cut your board into two equal lengths.

2. Lay one piece down and drive three nails in a straight line lengthwise down its center until they poke out through the opposite surface.

3. Stand the other board on its edge. Place the board with the nails on top of it to form a **T** shape. The protruding nails will help keep the pieces aligned.

4. Use the hammer to drive the nails into the on-edge board.

5. Turn your **T** upside down (nail heads down) and clamp it securely to your work surface.

To Make the Perfect Curl

6. Leaning over and exerting steady pressure, run your plane along the exposed edge of the board. Notice what happens.

Concentrate on the relationship between the pressure you exert and the look of the ribbonlike shaving that comes rippling out of the plane's throat. Try pushing a little harder; try letting up on the pressure. Move quickly and then a bit more slowly. Experiment until you have made the most perfect curl you can!

7. With a needle and white thread, you can easily turn your curls into delicate hangings for your window, Christmas tree, or chandelier. If you hang a few from a branch or twig, you can make a beautiful mobile.

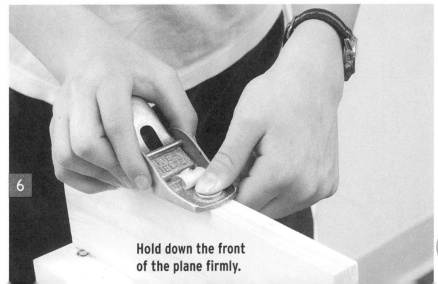

6

Hold down the front of the plane firmly.

Measuring

THE BASICS

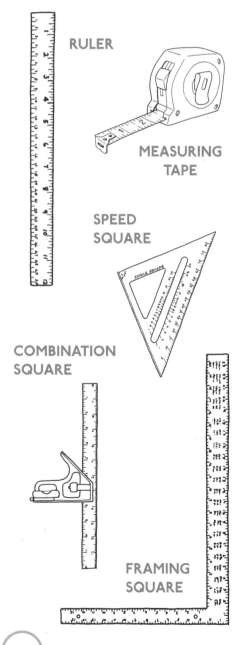

RULER

MEASURING TAPE

SPEED SQUARE

COMBINATION SQUARE

FRAMING SQUARE

I t can take a while for young carpenters to get to the point where they trust their own measuring and marking skills. Competence with measuring tools is a must for happy building, but only time and practice will bring about this contented state. This section describes some of the basic tools for measuring, as well as how to handle and use them to best effect.

The Measuring Tape and Ruler

The ruler is the simplest of measuring tools and is also a handy straightedge for drawing lines.

The retractable metal-bladed tape measure is the preferred measuring tool of most carpenters. It's used not as a straight-edge for drawing lines but as a tool to measure long lengths. One thing to note about the measuring tape is that the hooked end that is riveted onto the tape always seems loose. This motion compensates for the thickness of the tape end when you are making *inside* and *outside* measurements.

Push the end of the tape against the side to make an inside measurement (left). Hook the end and pull tight for an outside measurement (right).

Use squares for measuring, marking, and drawing lines.

Hold the flanged side of the Speed Square tight against edge of board.

Allegra uses a Speed Square to square a line across this wide board.

Three Squares

The Speed Square is a great tool. You can use it to measure short lengths or to *square a line* (draw a line at a 90-degree angle to one side of a board), but you can also use it to lay out lines at an angle. The Speed Square makes it especially easy to draw a square line because it has a lip, or flanged side, that rests firmly against the edge of a board. Use a tape measure to mark out lengths on a long board, but when it's time to draw an angled or a square line at those points, the Speed Square is the tool of choice.

The combination square is similar to the Speed Square, and it can be used for many of the same jobs. The basic difference is that its rule has measurements marked on it, and that rule is movable. By loosening a knob, you can reposition it to conve-

niently measure any distance from the edge of a board. The combination square also contains a level, which can come in really handy at times!

In the hands of an experienced carpenter, a steel framing square is an essential tool for complicated tasks like laying out rafters and stairs. Kids, however, are more likely to appreciate the framing square as a right-angled ruler. Because it has scales marked on all four of its long edges, the framing square is the perfect tool for measuring "over and in." You can measure 12 inches over from the end of a board, square a line to mark that length, and locate a point 4 inches in from the edge along that line — all in a single step!

The long side of a framing square measures 24 inches and is called the *body* or the *blade*. The

shorter side of the tool is 16 inches long and is called the *tongue*. The blade is 2 inches wide, while the tongue is 1½ inches wide; these widths correspond to the dimensions of rough-sawn and dressed lumber.

KEEPING TRACK OF SCALES

Always keep track of whether you are using the inside or the outside scales on the framing square. If you look at the scales stamped on the inside and outside of the tongue, you'll notice that they're offset by 2 inches (the width of the blade) from each other. Measuring along an outside scale and marking along an inside one is an easy error to make!

Hold the handle of the square against the edge of the board, slide the square to your mark (left), and draw the line against the blade of the square (right).

Squaring a Line

Squaring a line simply means drawing a line perpendicular (at a 90-degree angle) to a straight edge. In most cases, you'll square lines across a board.

To square a line, hold one edge of your square (the flanged side of the Speed Square, the handle of the combination square, or the body of the framing square) against the edge of your board. Slide the square until the upper corner (where the two sides of the square meet at a right angle) reaches the place where you want the line to begin and draw a line across the board there, keeping your pencil steady against the straight edge of the square.

Laying Out an Angled Line

Grasp the Speed Square by its flanged side. Align the corner (where the two short sides meet) with the point where you want your angled line to begin. Locate the reading for your desired angle on the scale stamped into the longest edge of the tool. Pivot the square until the correct mark lines up with the edge of the board. Draw off the angle against the top edge of the tool.

Direct Measurement

One of the best ways to handle any measurement task (without a lot of tools) is to place the piece you need to cut in the spot where it needs to fit and mark the required length on it directly. There will be no numbers or fractions of inches involved and no adding or subtracting to confuse you! When you are building a project from this book and one of your pieces has to fit in a particular spot, try marking it off directly, instead of relying on the calculated dimensions. You'll be following in the footsteps of professional carpenters like cabinetmakers and stairbuilders, who often create their own "ruler" of a room by marking lines on a length of board to indicate the position of windowsills, door edges, and electrical outlets.

Along the same lines, if you need multiple pieces of one part, it's possible that cutting one and using it as a pattern to cut the others will be simpler than measuring and marking each one.

Hold the flange against the edge of the board (1), then pivot the square until the correct scale reading meets the edge of the board and draw the line against the top of the square (2).

read angle here

The Paper Rule

The trouble with the measuring system we inherited from the English is how complex it is to use. Its basic premise is simple, however. A single unit, the inch — derived from the length of three grains of barley laid end to end — is divided in half, then simply divided again and again until we get to the 32nds of an inch marked on most rulers.

A good way for young carpenters to learn to understand the bewildering profusion of markings on a ruler is to make their own. In the process, they'll make a handy fraction reference.

Get a piece of unlined paper (approximately 8½ by 11 inches). Fold the paper in half lengthwise. Open it up and make a line along half the length of this crease and label it *1/2*. Now either side of this fold (from the line to the edge of the paper) represents half of the overall length of the paper. Fold in one of the outer edges so it aligns with the *1/2* mark in the center of the paper and crease it down. Open up the fold, mark about a quarter of the length of

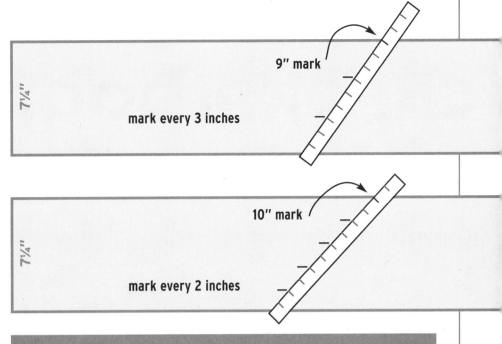

dividing a board into three parts (top) and five parts (bottom)

the crease, and label it *1/4*. Repeat this process on the opposite side of the page. Continue dividing the sheet by halves, working from the outside edges toward the last fraction you marked. The result will be a double-ended "ruler" that can be used to measure household objects in fractions of a sheet of paper. To measure an object that is more than half a page long, you'll have to add the fractions together to arrive at the correct length. It might be a bit confusing at first, but it's good measuring practice.

Dividing a Board into Equal Parts

This is a neat measuring trick. Let's say that we want to divide a 1x8 board into three equal widths. This board is actually 7¼ inches wide, so it's not a simple calculation! But there is a simple layout method for dividing any width into equal parts.

To divide a width into thirds (or three parts), we can use any multiple of three that is larger than the dimension to be divided. In our example, nine (3 x 3) is the first multiple of three larger than 7¼. Lay a square or a ruler on a diagonal across the width of the board so that the end of the ruler touches one edge and the 9-inch mark aligns with the other edge. Now make a mark at each 3-inch increment (3 inches and 6 inches). The distance from the edge of the board to the mark nearest that edge is one third the width of the board.

If you wanted instead to divide the board into five equal parts, you could use any multiple of five larger than 7¼. Fifteen would work, but ten (5 x 2) is the logical choice. Lay the ruler across the board with one end on one side and the 10-inch mark on the other and mark at every 2-inch increment. The illustration above shows these examples.

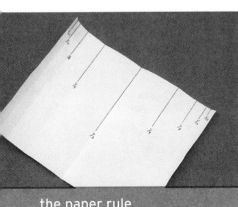

the paper rule

checkerboard

Practice your measuring and make a good rainy-day game at the same time! Traditional game boards are full of measured straight lines, and as you work on laying them out just right, your measuring and calculating skills will get sharper and sharper.

What You'll Need

MATERIALS

1x12 clear pine board (at least 1 foot long)

Paint in two colors of your choice

TOOLS

Handsaw

Block plane (optional)

Ruler (optional)

Framing square

Sandpaper

Paintbrush

How Big Are the Squares?

1. A checkerboard has eight squares along each of its sides. The board also needs a border around the "playing field." We will make it half the width of one square. This means the pine board needs to be divided into nine equal sections (eight squares plus two half-squares equals nine squares).

2. Our 1x12 pine board is 11¼ inches wide. To divide 11¼ inches into nine equal sections, we'll use the measuring trick you just read about (page 33). The first multiple of nine that is larger than 11¼ is 18 (9 x 2 = 18). Lay

a ruler or a framing square diagonally across the board, with the left end of the ruler or square at one edge of the board and the 18-inch mark on the opposite edge of the board. From the 18-inch mark, measure back 2 inches and make a mark on your board there. Pick up the ruler or square and use it to measure from the edge of the board to the mark. The distance should be 1¼ inches away. Now you know that one ninth of 11¼ inches is 1¼ inches. You have just used a ruler instead of a calculator to solve your math problem! Each square on the checkerboard will be 1¼ inches wide and 1¼ inches long.

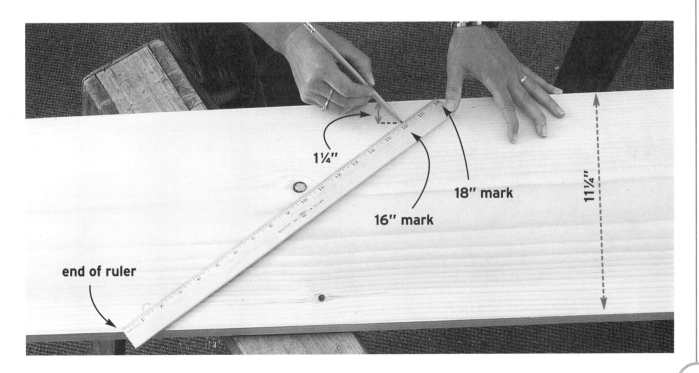

1¼"

18" mark

16" mark

11¼"

end of ruler

draw a cut line
along the
inside edge

3

7

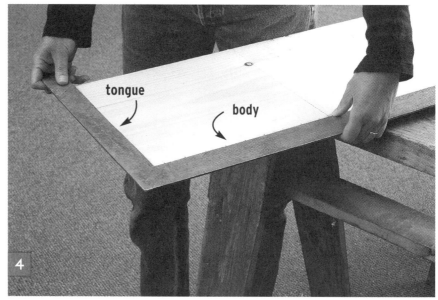

tongue

body

4

EASY ADDING

An easy trick when adding measurements is to add first the fraction and then the whole number. For example, the end of the first checkerboard square is at the 1⅞-inch mark on the framing square. The next mark has to be 1¼ inches farther along. To get there, first add the ¼ inch by moving two ⅛-inch lines down the scale. Read the mark on the scale that indicates your position (2⅛ inches). Then move the remaining inch (to 3⅛ inches) and make a mark there.

Laying Out the Board

3. Since the checkerboard is going to be 11¼ inches (the width of the pine board) square, we need to mark a cut line this distance from the end of the board. Hold the body of the framing square against the far edge of the board, with the end of the body pointing toward the end of the board and the tongue extending across the face of the board. Align the 11¼-inch mark on the inside edge of the square's body with the end of the board. Holding the square firmly in position, draw a line along the inside edge of the tongue. This single step should yield a nice square line at the proper dimension on the board.

4. Rotate the framing square so that the inside of the body rests against the far edge of the board and the inside of the tongue rests against the end of the board. Hold the square flush with the

face of the board so you will be able to make layout marks there.

5. The border around the checkerboard will be half the width of a square, or ⅝ inch wide. Starting from the inside corner of the square, make a mark on the board beside the ⅝-inch line on the square's tongue. This marks the edge of the border around the playing field.

6. Move 1¼ inches (1⅞ inches total) along the tongue and make a mark there; this marks the edge of the first square. Keep marking at 1¼-inch increments until you end up ⅝ inch short of the near edge of the board.

7. After you have completed the layout along the tongue of the square, return to the inside corner and repeat the measuring and marking process along the body. When you reach the cut line (the first line you drew), the layout is complete.

8

9

6. Slide the framing square along the face of the board until the inside of the tongue lies along the cut line. Repeat the measuring and marking process along the inside of the tongue, again beginning with a mark at ⅝ inch and then marking at 1¼-inch increments. Be sure not to make your marks along the outside edge of the tongue, because its scale is offset from the one on the inside of the tongue.

9. Use any side of the square as a straightedge to connect the measured points on the end of the board with the corresponding points on the cut line.

10. Align the inside of the square's body with the far edge of the board and the inside of the tongue with the cut line. Slide the framing square toward the end of the board, stopping at each mark you made along the far edge to square a line across the board.

11. Using a handsaw, cut along the cut line to free your game board from the pine board.

Finishing

12. If your board has any rough spots, sand them smooth. If you want, chamfer the edges of your board with a block plane.

13. Paint the squares in alternating colors. Who says that a checkerboard has to be black and red? You made the board, so you get to choose the color scheme!

to parents

You can create an old-fashioned incised effect on the checkerboard by cutting the layout lines into it with a utility knife. Position the framing square about ⅛ inch away from and parallel to one of the lines marking the border. Hold the utility knife at a 30-degree angle and slice into the wood along the edge of the square. You should be making one side of a V-shaped cut, with the center of the groove marking the former position of the line. Reposition the square on the opposite side of the line and make another angled cut to complete the groove.

Cut all the lines of the border first, followed by the lines of the grid within the border.

Allegra painted her checkerboard yellow and blue!

13

part

2

down to business:

building your own projects

string art

This project gives carpenters plenty of practice hammering, cutting, and measuring — and some quality stringing time, too! A beautiful work of art will result from careful measuring and planning, but an intriguing piece can also be made by free-form cutting, unplanned nailing, and wild abandon.

What You'll Need

TOOLS

Handsaw

Your favorite measuring tools

Hammer

Pencil

MATERIALS

Wood scraps

String or yarn

FASTENERS

Nails (4d galvanized box nails or shingle nails)

Camille says: "I loved this project! There's no end to all the patterns you can make. One of my projects used sixty nails! My sister Allegra is two years younger than I am and we both had fun, so this project isn't just for little kids — it's for big kids too!"

kids!

Getting Started

1. Grab a piece of wood that appeals to you. It can be any size, but the results will be better if it's at least 12 inches long.

2. If you want the board to be a different size or shape, cut it with a handsaw. You could also nail one or more pieces of wood together for a three-dimensional String Art sculpture.

To Measure or Not to Measure...

3. If you want to pursue a totally improvisational (free-form) course, skip ahead to step 5. Otherwise, use a pencil and a measuring tool — a ruler or square for straight lines or a compass for circles — to draw on the board a line (or lines) to mark the future placement of the nails.

4. On the line(s) you just drew, measure and mark at even intervals the exact locations where the nails will go.

Straight lines

To space nails evenly on a straight line, use a ruler or measuring tape, marking every ½ to 1 inch.

Circles

To space nails evenly around a circle, set a compass so that its two legs are ½ to 1 inch apart. Place the compass point on your circle line. Swing the pencil-holding leg of the compass around until the pencil crosses the circle line; make a mark there. Move the compass point to the mark you just made and make the next mark where the pencil now crosses the circle line. Repeat all the way around the circle. If the last marks are not perfectly spaced, adjust them by eye.

3

4

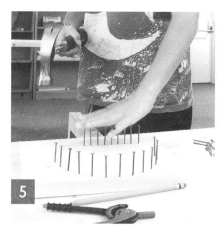  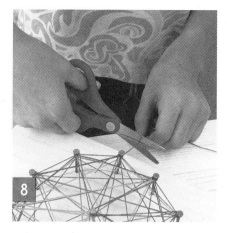

Grab Your Hammer

5. Drive nails at all the spots you've marked or, if you're making a free-form piece, wherever you like. Drive the nails just until they are firmly set in your board; don't hammer them all the way into the board. Make sure that, when you're done, the nail heads are all at about the same height.

Stringing

6. This is the finale! Tie your string firmly onto the first nail, close to the head. If you're stringing a circle, start with any nail. If you're stringing a line, start with a nail at the end of the line.

7. If you're working on a free-form piece, string away! If you're working on a symmetrical design, follow a stringing pattern, such as the Sunset, Sunshine, Arrow, or Double Bridge (see the diagrams on pages 44–45). Whichever pattern you decide on, be sure to keep the string pulled taut as you work.

8. When you're done, tie your string securely to the last nail and trim the ends of the string with scissors.

Wrap the strings any way you like! Here, Camille works on a three-dimensional Double Bridge pattern.

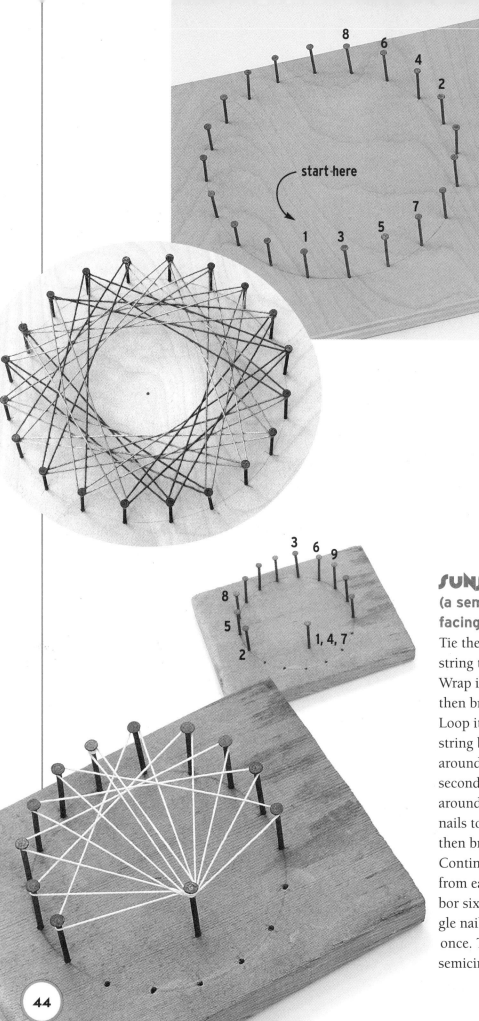

SUNSHINE
(nails in a circle):

Tie the string to any nail. Pull the string to a nail seven nails to the right of your starting nail. Wrap it once all the way around this nail, then bring it back to the nail just to the right of your starting nail. Wrap the string all the way around this nail and then pull it to the nail seven nails to its right. Again, wrap the string all the way around the nail and then head the string back to the nail just to the right of the previous nail. Proceed this way around the entire circle — seven forward, six back. (Seven is not a magic number; you can create this pattern skipping forward any number of nails you choose. Just pick a number and stick with it.)

SUNSET
(a semicircle of nails facing a single nail):

Tie the string to the single nail. Pull the string to the left-most nail of the semicircle. Wrap it once all the way around this nail, then bring it to a nail six nails to its right. Loop it around this nail, then bring the string back to the single nail. Loop the string around the single nail, then bring it to the second nail of the semicircle. Loop it once around this nail, then pull it to a nail six nails to its right. Loop it around this nail, then bring it back to the single nail. Continue in this fashion, working your way from each nail in the semicircle to its neighbor six nails away and then back to the single nail, until every nail has been looped once. Tie your string at the last nail in the semicircle or the single nail and you're done!

the arrow

(nails in a V shape):

Turn the board so the **V** is upside down. Tie the string to the last nail on the right-hand line. Then pull the string to the nail at the point of the **V** shape. Wrap the string once all the way around this nail, then bring it back to the next-to-last nail on the right-hand line. Wrap the string all the way around this nail, then pull it to the first-from-the-point nail on the left-hand line. Pull the string all the way around this nail and lead it back to the nail two places away from your starting nail. Continue this way, moving your string along one nail at a time down both lines.

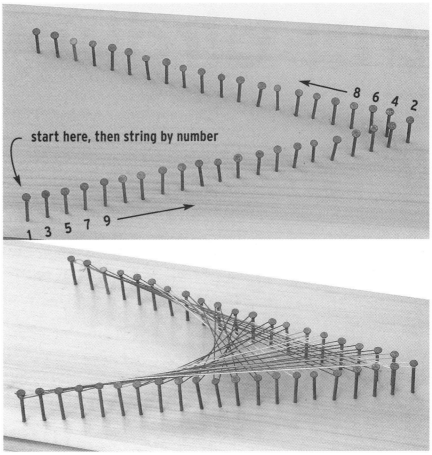

start here, then string by number

8 6 4 2

1 3 5 7 9

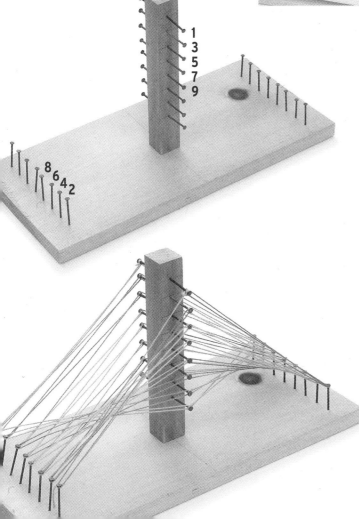

double bridge

(three-dimensional):

Tie your string to the top nail on one of the vertical rows of nails. Pull the string to the last nail on one of the horizontal rows on the same side of the board. Loop the string around this nail, then pull it to the nail second from the top on the vertical line. From there, go to second nail on the horizontal, back to the third nail on the vertical, and so on, until you have wrapped the string around all the nails on those horizontal and vertical rows. When you reach the end of the horizontal row, pull the string from the nail at the end of that row to the top nail on the other vertical row. Work your way back along the nails on the same horizontal row (each one already has a loop of string around it) until you reach the end. Now pull your string to the topmost nail on the first vertical row. Repeat the process along the other horizontal row until you are done!

twin birdHouse

This is a simple, quick, appealing project that yields hours of fun come springtime. A friend of ours and his sons built the first version of this birdhouse, turning leftover pieces of clapboard siding into a spiffy new house for the local bird population. We've modified their project a bit for this book, giving you the option of making either a back-to-back two-family birdhouse or a single-family residence. The instructions for the twin version start here; the single birdhouse instructions begin on page 52.

Measuring and Marking

1. Hook your tape measure on the right-hand end of the 1x6 pine board. Moving toward the left, mark points at 5 inches, 11 inches, 16 inches, 28 inches, and 33 inches. Square a line across the board at each of these points.

2. On the first two lines (5 inches and 11 inches from the right-hand end of the board), mark center points, which should be 2¾ inches in from either edge of the board. These will be the centers of the entrance holes you will drill later in front #1 and front #2.

3. From the point where the 5-inch line ends at the top of the board, use your Speed Square to draw a line down and toward the left at a 45-degree angle. From the bottom of the 5-inch line, draw a line up and toward the left at a 45-degree angle. Extend the lines until they intersect at the center of the board; this intersection point marks the top of gabled front #1 of the birdhouse.

4. Move down to the line at 11 inches. From both ends of this line, draw a line at a 45-degree

What You'll Need

TOOLS

Jigsaw or handsaw

Speed Square

Drill

¼-inch drill bit

1¼-inch Forstner bit

#6 countersink bit

Phillips-head screwdriver

Hammer

Tape measure

Carpenter's glue

Clamps

Safety glasses

MATERIALS

One 4-foot length of 1x6 #2 pine board

One 4-foot length of ½-inch x 6-inch cedar clapboard

¼-inch dowel or short piece of tree branch

Scrap wood

Paint (optional)

FASTENERS

Six 1¼-inch drywall screws

One package 1-inch brads

angle headed to the right, toward the first set of angled lines. The intersection of these two lines marks the top of gabled front #2.

5. Move down to the last line (33 inches from the end). From both ends of this line, draw a line at a 45-degree angle headed to the left, toward the end of the board. The intersection of these two lines marks the top of the gable of the center partition.

6. Put the 1¼-inch bit in the drill chuck. Clamp the board down on top of a length of scrap wood. Starting the spur of the bit at the center point you marked on the first line at the right-hand end of the board, drill all the way through the piece and into the scrap to make the first entrance hole to the house. Then move to the center point on the second line and drill another hole for the second entrance.

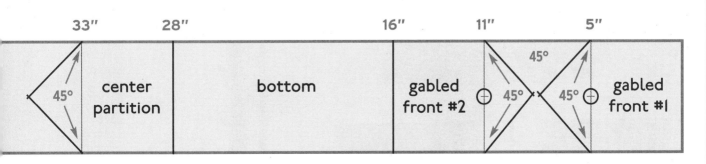

Cutting Out the Pieces

7. Clamp the board down so that the right-hand end extends at least 12 inches beyond the work surface. Use a jigsaw or handsaw to make the two cuts along the first set of angled lines. This will free the birdhouse front #1 from the workpiece.

8. Cut along the next set of angled lines on the right-hand end of the board. Then turn the board around, reclamp it, and cut along the angled lines on the other end. Make the two crosscuts along the remaining layout lines. These cuts will free up the birdhouse front #2, the bottom, and the center partition. *Note:* Do not cut along any layout lines that intersect angled cuts! They are for locating the entrance holes only.

9. On the length of clapboard, measure and square lines to mark two 12-inch-long pieces for the birdhouse sides and two 13-inch-long pieces to make the roof pieces. Cut them to length and set them aside.

10. On the birdhouse bottom, mark a point in each corner, about 1 inch in from the closest side and about ⅜ inch in from the closest end.

11. Square a line 6 inches in from one end of the bottom. Mark two points along this line, about 1 inch from either edge.

12. Put the countersink bit in the drill chuck and use it to drill a hole at each of the six spots you've marked on the birdhouse bottom.

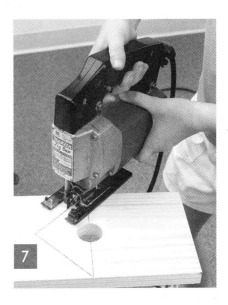

7

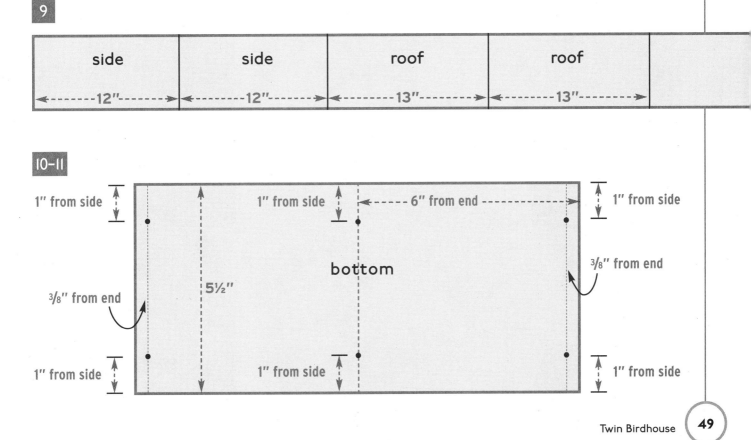

9

side	side	roof	roof	
12"	12"	13"	13"	

10–11

1" from side · 1" from side · 6" from end · 1" from side

⅜" from end · bottom · ⅜" from end

5½"

1" from side · 1" from side · 1" from side

to parents

A word about materials: Cedar clapboards are manufactured with one side planed smooth and the other left rough-sawn, so the two sides have very different feels. Which way you position them could ultimately create quite different effects. Although we've specified pine board for the rest of the birdhouse, you can make it out of cedar instead and leave it to weather naturally outdoors. So before you begin building, you and your kids have a basic design decision to make: What will the neighborhood birds prefer — a rough-hewn cabin or a summer cottage?

Putting It All Together

13. Set front #1, front #2, and the center partition in a row on edge on the work surface, with their peaks pointing away from you. Place the birdhouse bottom on edge against the bottom edges of the two fronts and the center partition, with the countersunk holes facing you.

14. Align the center partition with the holes in the center of the bottom piece and drive two 1¼-inch drywall screws through the holes into the bottom edge of the partition. Align one front piece with the holes in the end of the bottom piece and drive screws through the holes to fasten these

two pieces together. Repeat the process with the other front piece. (Using screws instead of nails will allow you to remove the bottom for cleaning after the birdhouse's first inhabitants have moved on.)

15. With the assembly still lying on its side, place one of the 12-inch pieces of clapboard against the side of the birdhouse, with its thick edge at the bottom. Using two or three brads at each location, nail the clapboard onto the two fronts and the center of the birdhouse. Don't get carried away and nail the clapboard to the bottom. That would become a sure source of consternation at clean-out time!

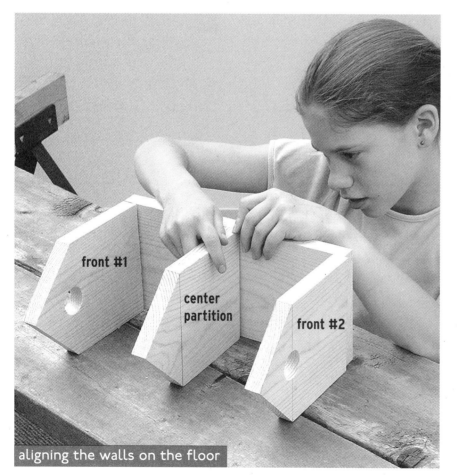

front #1

center partition

front #2

aligning the walls on the floor

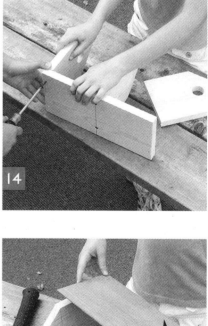

14

15

thick edge at bottom

16. Turn the birdhouse over and nail the second piece of 12-inch clapboard to the other side in the same way.

17. Set the house upright and place one of the 13-inch clapboard roof pieces on top of the walls, with its thin edge at the peak. The clapboard will hang over the ends of the walls by about half an inch. Nail the roof piece in place by driving two brads through the roof into the center and two front pieces.

18. Place the second 13-inch roof piece in place, with its thin edge flush to the surface of the first roof piece (this will make it harder for rain to enter). Drive two brads through the roof into the center and two front pieces.

The Perch

19. If you want to include a perch, put the ¼-inch bit in your drill chuck. Bore into one of the fronts of the birdhouse about ¾ inch below the bottom edge of the entry hole. The hole should be about ½ inch deep.

hammer gently to avoid splitting the clapboard

attaching the roof

20. Cut a 3-inch length of ¼-inch dowel, roll one end in a bit of carpenter's glue, and push or tap it into the hole you just drilled. If you prefer to use a short length of tree branch for a perch, simply cut it to length and shape the end with a knife until it fits into the drilled hole.

21. If you want to have perches on both fronts of the birdhouse, repeat steps 19 and 20 on the other house front.

Finishing

22. Paint polka dots, stripes, or any pattern you think the neigborhood birds might like! However, because this is an outdoor birdhouse, make sure you paint with waterproof, preferably semigloss or gloss paint. If you have made your birdhouse entirely from cedar, consider not painting at all, letting the weather do the finish work for you naturally.

thin edge at top
18

19

a tap will do it
20

single birdhouse

Why make a single-family birdhouse rather than a two-family? This version is no simpler or more difficult to build than the Twin Birdhouse (page 46), but perhaps the birds in your neighborhood would prefer a little more privacy!

Measuring and Marking

1. Hook your tape measure on the right-hand end of the 1x6 board. Moving toward the left, mark points at 4 inches, 9 inches, 18 inches, and 23 inches. Square a line across the board at each of these points.

2. Mark the center point, which should be 2¾ inches in from either edge of the board, of the first line (4 inches from the right-hand end of the board). This will be the center of the entrance hole you will drill later.

3. From the point where the 4-inch line ends at the top of the board, use your Speed Square to draw a line down and toward the right at a 45-degree angle. From the bottom of the 4-inch line, draw a line up and toward the right at a 45-degree angle. Extend the lines until they intersect at the center of the board; this intersection marks the top of the gabled front piece of the birdhouse.

4. Move down to the last line (23 inches from the end). Repeat the layout of step 3 to draw two

lines heading to the left at a 45-degree angle and intersecting at the center of the board; this intersection marks the top of the gabled back of the birdhouse.

5. Put the 1¼-inch bit in the drill chuck. Clamp the board down on top of a length of scrap wood. Start the spur of the bit at the center point you marked on the first line and drill all the way through the piece into the scrap.

What You'll Need

TOOLS

Jigsaw or handsaw

Speed Square

Drill

¼-inch drill bit

1¼-inch Forstner bit

#6 countersink bit

Screwdriver

Hammer

Tape measure

Carpenter's glue

Clamps

Safety glasses

MATERIALS

One 4-foot length of 1x6 #2 pine board

One 4-foot length of ½-inch x 6-inch cedar clapboard

¼-inch dowel or short piece of tree branch

Scrap wood

Paint (optional)

FASTENERS

Four 1¼-inch drywall screws

One package 1-inch brads

to parents

You can use a metal or wooden bracket to mount your birdhouse to a tree or on a wall. Four to 6 feet off the ground should do it.

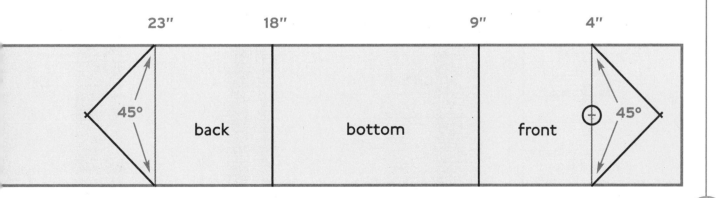

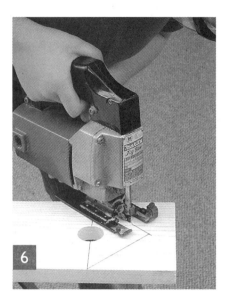

6

Cutting Out the Pieces

6. Clamp the board down so that the right-hand end extends beyond your work surface. Use a jigsaw or handsaw to cut along the two angled lines of the gabled front piece.

7. Turn the board around and make the angled cuts for the gabled back piece. Then make the two crosscuts along the lines in the center of the board (at 9 and 18 inches). *Note:* Do not cut along the two layout lines at either end of the board! These are only for marking the ends of the gables.

8. On the length of clapboard, measure and square lines to make two 9-inch-long pieces for the birdhouse sides and two 10-inch-long pieces for the roof. Cut them to length and set them aside.

9. On the birdhouse bottom, mark a point in each corner, about 1 inch in from the closest side and about ⅜ inch in from the closest end.

KEEPING IT CLEAN

Single or double, your birdhouse will require a small amount of annual home maintenance. In the fall, clean it out! Remove all twigs, feathers, and debris left behind by last year's tenants. In the spring, clean with soap and water, and pour boiling water over all surfaces to kill any parasites that might be claiming squatters' rights.

10. Put the countersink bit in the drill chuck and use it to drill a hole at each of the four spots you've marked on the birdhouse bottom.

8

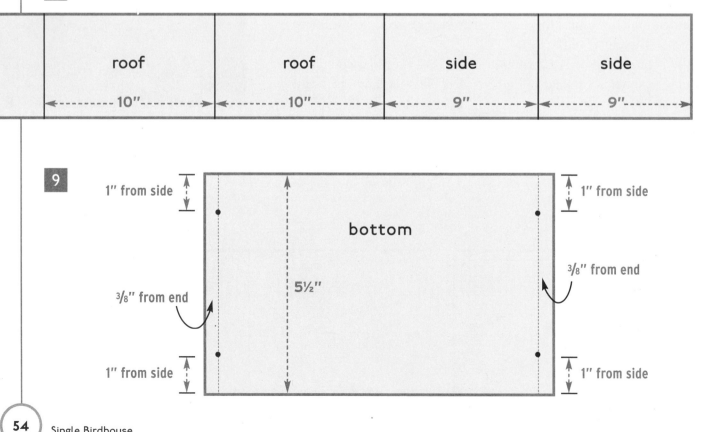

front

back

aligning the walls with the floor

12

Putting It All Together

11. Set the front and the back on edge on the work surface, with their peaks pointing away from you. Place the birdhouse bottom on edge against the bottom edges of the front and back, with the countersunk holes facing you.

12. Align the end of the bottom with the face of the front and drive two 1¼-inch drywall screws through the holes and into the front piece. Repeat the process to align and fasten the bottom to the back.

13. With the assembly still lying on its side, place one of the 9-inch pieces of clapboard against the side of the birdhouse, with its thick edge at the bottom. Using two or three brads on each end, nail the clapboard to the front and back of the birdhouse. Do not nail the clapboard to the bottom piece!

14. Turn the birdhouse over and nail the other 9-inch length of clapboard on the opposite side in the same way.

15. Set the house upright and place one of the 10-inch clapboard roof pieces on top of the walls, with its thin edge at the peak. The clapboard will hang over the ends of the walls by about half an inch. Nail the roof piece in place by driving two brads through the roof into the front and back pieces.

16. Place the second roof piece with its thin edge flush to the top surface of the first roof piece. Drive two brads through each end of the roof into the front and back of the birdhouse.

Finishing Touches

17. To finish the birdhouse with a perch and coat of paint, see steps 19 through 22 for the Twin Birdhouse (page 51).

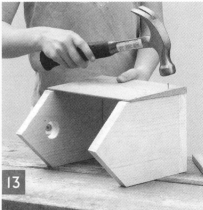

13

15

16

sturdy stool

We tried standing on this sturdy little piece of furniture in every corner and in every odd posture you can imagine and still it wouldn't tip over.

When Craig built the prototype for this project, Allegra looked at it and announced, "It makes our old one look bad." She was right. This stool makes all the rest look shoddy, and it makes all others seem tippy, too.

Measuring and Layout

1. Place the board on your work surface. Square a line 16 inches from the right-hand end. In that 16-inch-long space, measure 10 inches in from one of the long sides of the board in a couple of places. Using a straightedge, draw a line through the two marks, parallel to the edge of the board, from the end of the board to the line at 16 inches.

2. Square a line across the board at 18 inches, 28 inches, 38 inches, and 48 inches from the same end. Mark all these lines with an A for "angle." (You will be making bevel, or angled, cuts along these lines.)

3. Measure to the middle of the board (5⅝ inches) at a couple of points and draw a centerline from the line at 18 inches through the line at 38 inches.

4. Move to the left-hand end of the board. Draw a line parallel to the near side of the board, about

What You'll Need

TOOLS

Jigsaw or handsaw

Ruler, framing square, or combination square

Speed Square

Drill

⅛-inch drill bit

½-inch Forstner bit

Phillips-head screwdriver

Block plane or sandpaper

Measuring tape

Clamps

Safety glasses

MATERIALS

One 6-foot length of ¾ x 12 #2 pine board

½-inch wooden plugs

Carpenter's wood glue

Primer (optional)

Semigloss or satin paint (optional)

FASTENERS

2-inch drywall screws

1⅝-inch drywall screws

18 inches long and 3½ inches away from the edge. Use a Speed Square to draw a line at a 15-degree angle that starts at the edge of the board and intersects the parallel line. From this point of intersection, measure 10 inches along the parallel line and mark that point. Using the Speed

Square again, draw a line that starts at the edge of the board and intersects the parallel line at the spot you just marked, at a 15-degree angle opposite the first one. The lines will create a rhombus with its base along the edge of the board and a top edge 10 inches long. This is the stretcher.

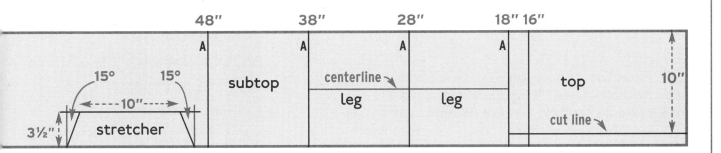

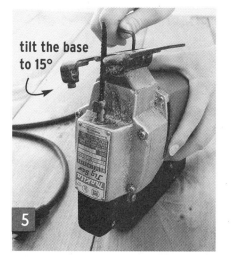

tilt the base
to 15°

5

to parents

This project calls for a lot of beveled cuts. Without good bevels, your sturdy stool will be anything but. If your kids are beginning carpenters, you may want to read ahead and prepare to make the bevel cuts yourself with a circular saw. The cuts will go more quickly, and they're likely to be more accurate.

Bevel Cuts

5. If you're using a jigsaw, tilt its base to cut at a 15-degree angle. If you're working with a handsaw, review the instructions for making a bevel cut on pages 14–15. When you make these cuts, make sure that the layout line is centered in the saw kerf. (A carpenter calls this "splitting the line.")

6. Make the first bevel cut at the 18-inch mark, with the saw angled toward the long portion of the board. The piece that is cut free is the stool top. The beveled end will be trimmed off later.

7. The next two cuts, at the 28-inch and the 38-inch marks, should be made with the saw angled in the same direction as in the previous cut. These two pieces are the legs of the stool. Do not cut at the 16-inch mark yet!

8. The fourth cut, for the subtop, is made with the saw blade angled in the opposite direction. Before you cut, look to make sure that the long point of the bevel will be on the top of the board. Then make the cut and free the subtop from the end of the board.

Square Cuts

9. If you are using a jigsaw, reset the blade to cut at a 90-degree angle.

10. Clamp the top piece to your work surface. Crosscut it to its 16-inch length along the line you have already drawn. Then rotate the board, clamp it down, and rip it along the line parallel to the edge. Use sandpaper to make the edges and top nice and smooth. You can use a plane to chamfer the edges for a more finished look.

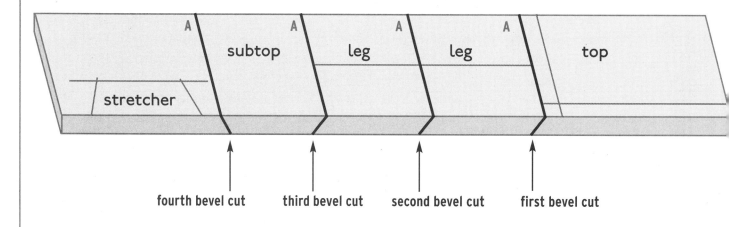

stretcher   subtop   leg   leg   top

fourth bevel cut   third bevel cut   second bevel cut   first bevel cut

Don't forget that the fourth bevel cut is made in the opposite direction from the first three! You may need to walk around the board and make this cut from the other side.

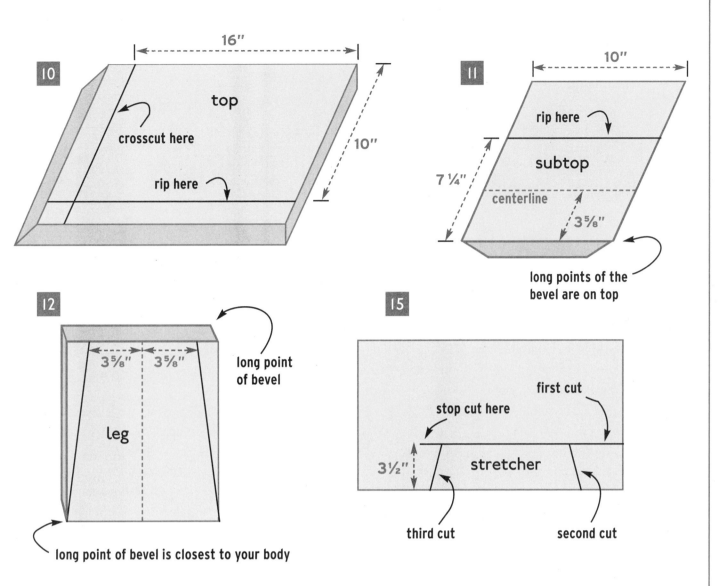

10 top — 16" — crosscut here — rip here — 10"

11 10" — rip here — subtop — 7 ¼" — centerline — 3⅝" — long points of the bevel are on top

12 3⅝" 3⅝" — long point of bevel — leg — long point of bevel is closest to your body

15 first cut — stop cut here — stretcher — 3½" — third cut — second cut

11. Lay the subtop flat so that the long points of the beveled ends are on top. Measure 7¼ inches in from one edge in two places, then use a straightedge to connect the two marks, drawing a line parallel to the edge and running the length of the piece. Clamp the piece and rip along this line. Then measure 3⅜ inches from one edge in two places and draw a centerline the length of the piece. Set the subtop aside.

12. Place one of the leg pieces with the centerline facing up and oriented so that the long point of the bevel is closest to your body.

Starting from the centerline, measure along the short point of the bevel 3⅜ inches to the left and to the right along the top edge of the board and mark these two points. Connect each of these points with its respective lower corner to make a rhombus.

13. Lay out the other leg in the same way.

14. Clamp the leg pieces down and cut along all four lines to create the finished legs.

15. Clamp the remainder of the board to your work surface

and make the three cuts to complete the stretcher piece. This will be easiest and safest if you leave the piece attached to the main length of board for as long as possible while you cut it out. Rip along the top edge first, cutting an inch or two past the corner of the piece. Then make the angled cut near the end, again cutting past the corner. Finally, make the opposite angle cut, running the saw past the corner until the piece drops free.

16. Use your block plane or sandpaper to smooth the rough spots on your sawed edges.

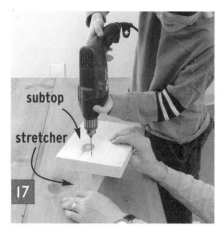

Putting It All Together

17. Gather the stretcher, the subtop, and your drill and screwdriver. Stand the stretcher upright with its longest side resting on the worktable. Lift the subtop and balance it on top of the stretcher. The long points of the subtop should align with the shoulders of the stretcher. Check that the overhang is the same on either side. At evenly spaced locations opposite the penciled centerline, drill three pilot holes using a ⅛-inch drill bit. Drill through the subtop down into the stretcher as far as the bit will travel. Then drive a 2-inch drywall screw into each hole and tighten it until the head is slightly recessed below the surface of the board.

18. Bring the two legs to your work surface. Lay them down with the centerline facing up and the short ends facing away from you. On the centerline, mark two points, one 2 inches and the other 4 inches from the top edge. Along the top edge of the leg, mark two more points, one 2 inches to the left and one 2 inches to the right of the centerline, about ¾ inch down from the shoulder.

19. Fit the Forstner bit in the drill chuck. Drill about ⅜ inch deep at the four points you just marked. This is called counter-boring a hole. After a screw is driven in, each recess will be concealed by a wooden plug.

20. Fit the ⅛-inch bit in the drill chuck. Clamp the T-shaped piece you assembled in step 17 to your work surface, upside down and with one end close to the edge of the work surface. Place one of the legs upside

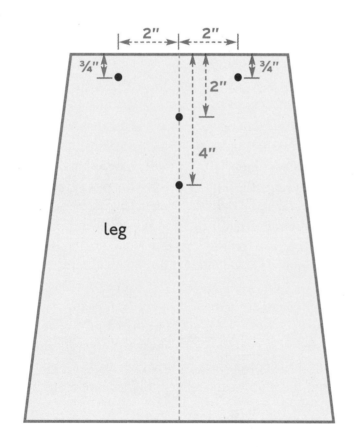

leg layout

22

23

24 Plug away!

down against one end of the assembly. The angled short end, or top, of the leg should rest snugly against the work surface. Drill through one of the counterbored holes along the centerline and into the end of the stretcher, starting the bit in the depression left by the spur of the Forstner bit. Drive a screw into this hole and tighten it to hold the alignment in place. Drill another pilot hole into the second counterbored hole along the centerline and drive another screw into the stretcher. Then drill two pilot holes in the counterbored holes along the top edge of the leg, into the subtop, and drive screws into both holes.

21. Unclamp the assembly, turn it around, and repeat the work of step 20 to attach the other leg.

22. Find the stool top and place it with its best face against the work surface. Place the rest of the stool assembly upside down on top of it. Center the assembly by measuring from both sides and ends to the edges of the top. When you have it just

right, mark the location of the edges on the top piece in case the pieces shift during drilling.

23. Drill pilot holes about 1½ inches deep (make sure you don't drill too deep) through each corner of the subtop into the stool top. Drive a 1⅜-inch drywall screw into each hole.

24. Bring the glue and wood plugs to your work area. Spread some glue on a piece of scrap wood. Roll the edges of a wood plug in the glue, then push the

plug into one of the counterbored holes. Keep plugging until all the counterbored holes are filled. After the glue is dry, use a block and sandpaper to sand the plugs flush.

Finishing

25. If you decide to paint your stool, be sure to apply primer first, followed by multiple coats of semigloss or satin paint. Camille traced her footprints on heavy paper and used them as a stencil for our stool top.

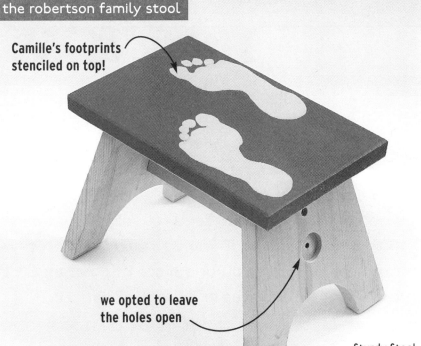

the robertson family stool

Camille's footprints stenciled on top!

we opted to leave the holes open

cricket cage

Cricket cages have been made for thousands of years in eastern Asia, where crickets are believed to bring good luck and intelligence; harming a cricket is thought to lead to great misfortune!

This cage can be a temporary home to any little critter, but it is especially suitable for a visiting cricket. We find a lot of curious bugs and animals, and we like to keep them around for a few days of study before we release them back into their own habitat. If you do take in a cricket, you can feed him rolled oats, potato, chunks of carrot, or a piece of an orange. Crickets also like to hide, so put in a few curly leaves or a piece of bark.

Making the Cage Top and Bottom

1. From the 1x6 board, cut two pieces that are each 7 inches long and 4⅜ inches wide.

2. Select one of these pieces to be the top of your cage. On the less attractive side of this piece, draw a line ½ inch in from each of the four edges. Starting at any point where the lines meet, make a small mark every ⅜ inch along each line. If you have measured and cut accurately, you should be able to make 15 marks along the long sides and 8 marks on the short sides. If your marks are not perfectly even, you can adjust them a little by eye.

3. The other piece will be the cage bottom. On the nicer side, draw a line ½ inch in from the edge on the two long sides and on only one of the short ends. (The unmarked end is where the door bottom will rest.) Make a small mark every ⅜ inch along these lines, the same way you did for the cage top.

4. Take a good look at your measured and marked top and bottom pieces. With the exception of one short end on your bottom piece, they should be marked identically.

5. With an awl, make starting holes for the drill at every small mark and at the corners on the top and the bottom pieces.

What You'll Need

TOOLS	MATERIALS
Handsaw	1x6 board (at least 2 feet long)
Fine finish saw or hacksaw	Five 48-inch lengths of ⅛-inch dowel
Ruler, Speed Square, or combination square	Carpenter's wood glue
Drill	Masking tape
⁹⁄₆₄-inch drill bit	One or two toothpicks
¹¹⁄₆₄-inch drill bit	Parting bead (⅜" x ¾" or other thin molding, at least 9 inches long)
Clamps	Scrap wood
Allen wrench	
Awl	
One sheet of 120-grit sandpaper	

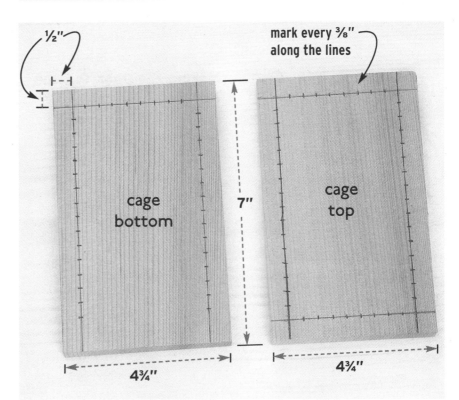

½"

mark every ⅜" along the lines

cage bottom

7"

cage top

4¾"

4¾"

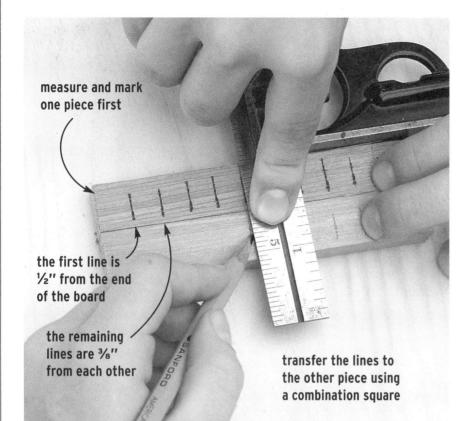

measure and mark one piece first

the first line is ½" from the end of the board

the remaining lines are ⅜" from each other

transfer the lines to the other piece using a combination square

7

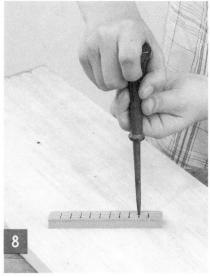

8

kids!

Camille says: "One reason that crickets are held in such high esteem is for their 'song,' or chirping. Only male crickets actually chirp. Try this out: Once you have a little cricket in your cage, count the number of times he chirps in a minute, divide by four, and add thirty-seven. This will tell you the temperature of the air in degrees Fahrenheit!"

Making the Door Top and Bottom

6. From the parting bead or molding, cut two lengths that are each 4⅜ inches long. These will be the top and bottom pieces of the door.

7. On one door piece, make a mark ½ inch in from each edge, and then make a mark every ⅜ inch between the two marks. You should be able to make ten evenly spaced marks. Lay the two door pieces next to each other and, using your combination square, draw a line across both pieces at each mark. This job is most easily done by two people together: one person

holding the combination square and the other drawing the lines.

6. With an awl, make starting holes for the drill in the center of every line you've drawn on one of the pieces. You can probably judge where the center of this very narrow piece of wood is by eye, but if you prefer, you can measure. This piece will be the door bottom.

9. On the other piece, skip the lines at each end and make holes with the awl at the center of the other eight lines. This piece will be the door top.

Cutting the Dowels

10. Using a finish saw or hacksaw, measure and cut your dowels into forty-two pieces that are each 4 inches long and eight pieces that are each 4½ inches long. Keep the different lengths in two separate piles! Put a rubber band around each group of same-size dowels and set them aside.

Drilling

11. Prepare the ⁵⁄₆₄-inch bit by wrapping a piece of masking tape around it so that ½ inch of the bit extends beyond the tape. Then put the bit in the drill chuck.

12. Clamp the top and bottom pieces of your cage to your work surface. Carefully drill at each awl mark just until the tape reaches the surface of the wood. The tape marks the depth you want the drill bit to penetrate. Don't exert too much pressure or you will drill too deep.

13. Now get out your top and bottom door pieces and clamp them to your work surface. Reset the tape so that about ¼ inch of the drill bit extends

beyond it, then drill a hole at each awl mark.

14. Put the ¹¹⁄₆₄-inch drill bit in the drill chuck. Clamp the bottom door piece to your work surface and drill all the way through the two holes at the ends. The bars of the door will slide through these larger holes.

15. Now find the cage top piece and clamp it to your work surface. Use the larger bit to drill all the way through all the holes *except* the corner holes along one of the short ends.

16. Sand all the pieces you have drilled to remove any burrs (rough spots) created by the drill and to get rid of pencil lines. Tap your pieces vigorously to get sawdust out of the holes.

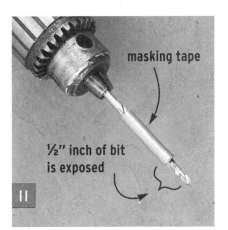

masking tape

½" inch of bit is exposed

11

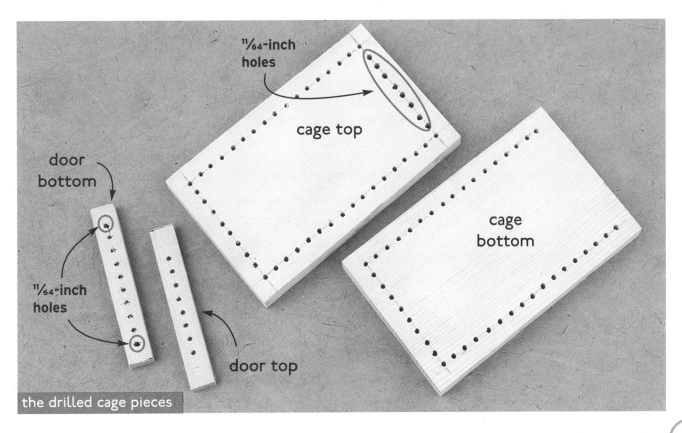

¹¹⁄₆₄-inch holes

cage top

door bottom

¹¹⁄₆₄-inch holes

door top

cage bottom

the drilled cage pieces

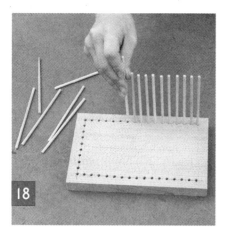 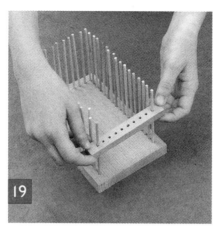 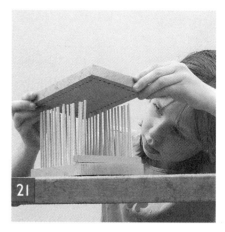

Assembling the Cage

17. Get out the 4-inch dowels, the bottom piece of the cage, some glue, and a piece of scrap wood. Make a little puddle of glue on the scrap wood. Dip the tip of a dowel in the glue so that it covers the end and a little bit of the sides. Insert the gluey end of the dowel into a hole in the cage bottom, push it all the way in, and adjust it so it stands up straight.

Camille says: "Putting in the dowels was very satisfying; the pieces of wood began to make sense and the cricket cage took shape. I liked rolling the dowels in glue and sticking them in the holes. The work went really quickly and the dowels looked cool when the cage was done."

kids!

18. Keep gluing and fitting dowels until all the holes are filled.

19. Hold the door bottom with its row of holes facing up. Thread the dowels that are in the corners of the open end of the cage bottom through the larger holes at either end of the door bottom. If the door bottom binds against the dowels, sand it until it slides freely.

20. Now grab your cage top and use a toothpick to put a nice dab of glue into each of the smaller-diameter holes in the piece. (Do not put glue in any of the holes that are drilled all the way through.)

21. To ease the dowels into the top piece without displacing them from the bottom, you will need four or more hands, all working patiently together. Carefully turn over the cage top and gently rest it over the dowels set in the bottom piece, lining up the dowels with the holes in the top piece. Starting at one corner, urge each dowel into the corresponding hole

in the cage top. Keep pressure on the top, and as each dowel is aligned the top will begin to slip into position. Kids' fingers can easily grasp the dowels, but adults may want to use an extra dowel to help push them in place.

22. When your cage has a top and bottom, you are almost done! Now you need to put the door together. With your toothpick, dab glue into the holes in the door bottom piece that is already part of the cage. Then thread your 4½-inch dowels through the holes in the cage top and down into the glue-filled holes in the door bottom.

23. Finally, while one person holds the bottom of the door about an inch above the cage bottom, the other builder must dab glue on the tops of the dowels that protrude above the top of the cage. Slide the dowels into the holes on the door top. Gently squeeze the door, from the top and bottom, to push the dowels as far into the holes as they can go. Slide your door up and down. You did it!

Working with friends
makes lining up the
pieces easier

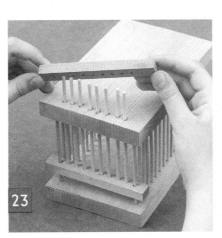

Finishing

24. All of the exterior surfaces
of your cage are suitable for painting. The interior will eventually
be covered by leaves and twigs.
We recommend leaving the bars
and interior bare. Remember, this
cage will be a temporary home for
your visiting cricket, so make
sure it's welcoming!

perfect toolbox

C raig learned most of his carpentry skills from a builder who carried his hand tools in an old toolbox that looked a lot like this one. When Craig built one for himself, he used the same design, making his out of recycled trim boards. Many of his carpenters carry similar toolboxes. When it came time to design toolboxes for our kids, we just scaled down the size a little and went with the tried-and-true model presented here.

What You'll Need

TOOLS

Speed Square

Framing square or straightedge

Handsaw

Phillips-head screwdriver

Electric drill

1¼-inch Forstner or paddle drill bit

¼-inch drill bit

Countersink bit

Four clamps

Wood mallet or hammer

Block plane

MATERIALS

One 6-foot length of 1x6 pine board

One 6-foot length of 1x10 pine board

One 3-foot length of 1¼-inch hardwood dowel

100-grit sandpaper

Carpenter's wood glue

Wood scrap with at least one straight edge

Weatherproof finish (such as polyurethane)

Paintbrush

FASTENERS

One pound 2-inch drywall screws (you will have some left over)

Pencil Work

1. On the 1x6 board, square a line 24 inches in from each end. These two 24-inch sections will become the sides of your toolbox. The leftover portion in the middle of the board will be scrap.

2. On the 1x10 board, square a line 12 inches in from each end. These two 12-inch sections will become the end pieces of your toolbox.

3. On the 1x10 board, square a line 24 inches away from one of the lines you just drew. This 24-inch section will become the bottom of the toolbox.

4. On one end of the 1x10 board, make a small mark on one edge 5¾ inches in from the end. Repeat on the opposite edge of the board (you can use a framing square to make a matching mark directly across from the first one).

5. Find the center of the end of the board and make a small mark there. From this point, measure 1 inch to the left and 1 inch to the right along the end of the board and mark those points. Using the framing square or a straightedge, draw a line connecting these points with the 5¾-inch marks on either edge of the board. These lines will become the sloped sides of your toolbox ends.

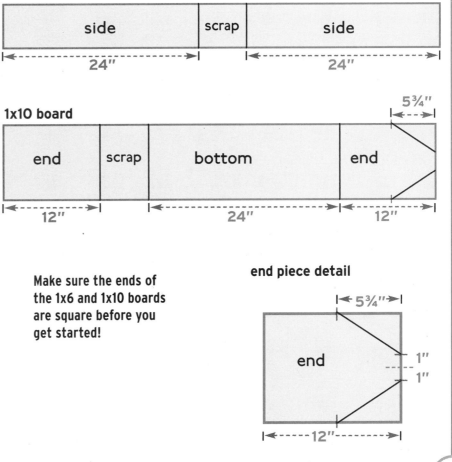

1x6 board

| side | scrap | side |

← 24" → ← 24" →

1x10 board

5¾"

| end | scrap | bottom | end |

← 12" → ← 24" → ← 12" →

Make sure the ends of the 1x6 and 1x10 boards are square before you get started!

end piece detail

← 5¾" →

end

1"
1"

← 12" →

scrap
wood

Keep the
blade against
the guide

6. Place the flange of the Speed Square against one of the long edges of the 1x10 board, near the end you are working on. Set your pencil on the center mark and slide the Speed Square up to it. Pull the square and the pencil together down the length of the board, drawing a center-line a couple of inches long.

7. Measure 1½ inches from the end of the board along your centerline and mark this point. This point will be the center of the hole you'll drill later for the tool-box handle.

8. Repeat steps 4 through 7 on the other end of the 1x10 board.

Making the Cuts

9. Place the 1x10 board on your work surface so that about 1 foot of board extends beyond the surface. Clamp the board to the work surface.

10. Place a piece of scrap wood along the inside of the angled cut line, so you can just see the line. Clamp the scrap wood in place; this will be a guide for your saw.

11. Position yourself at the end of the board so that the angled cuts are converging toward you. When you cut from this position, the saw will follow the grain of

the wood. Keeping the saw blade riding against the guide board, make the first angled cut.

12. Move the scrap-wood guide to the second angled line at the end of the board and make the second cut there.

13. Move the scrap-wood guide to the line you squared across the board 12 inches from the end and crosscut the board along that line.

14. Flip the board around so that its other end extends from the work surface. Repeat steps 11, 12, and 13 to complete the other end piece.

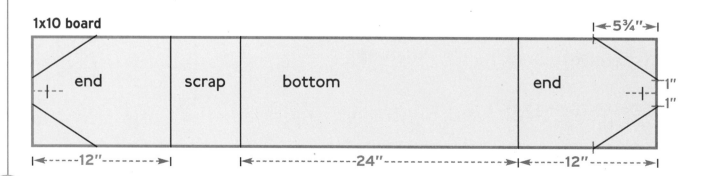

1x10 board

end   scrap   bottom   end

5¾"

1"
1"

12"   24"   12"

15. Double-check the measurement from the end of the board to the cut line for the bottom piece. It should be 24 inches. Redraw the line if necessary. Then reposition the scrap-wood guide and make the crosscut.

16. Using the scrap-wood guide, crosscut the two sides from the 1x6 board.

17. Cut your wooden dowel to 26½ inches.

Drilling

18. Place a piece of scrap wood under one of the end pieces and clamp both to the work surface.

19. Put the 1¼-inch Forstner or paddle bit in the drill chuck. Holding the drill as vertical as possible, drill a hole at the center point you marked earlier, through the end piece and into the scrap.

20. Drill the other end piece in the same manner.

to parents

Your kids will be using a large drill bit to drill through the end piece, and there will be a lot of resistance as it turns. If the end piece is not held firmly and the bit grabs, the wood will spin with the drill, so be sure to clamp the end piece. Large drill bits can also bind in the hole and cause the drill to twist suddenly. An adult should help brace the tool.

drilling a hole for the handle

Align the end and bottom at the edge of your work surface

Assembly

21. Take a minute to match up the pieces and double-check their sizes. The sides and the bottom should be the same length but different widths. The two ends should match and the holes in them should line up. If the saw cuts are a little ragged, clean them up with a block plane or coarse sandpaper.

22. Assembly of the toolbox will go better with extra hands to hold things in position while they are being aligned, drilled, or fastened. If another person is not available, we advise the liberal and creative use of clamps to hold the toolbox parts still. Place the bottom piece, better side facing up, near the edge of your work surface. Set one end piece, better side facing outward, in place against the bottom piece. Align the edges of both pieces and set them at the outermost edge of your work surface.

23. Put the countersink bit in the drill chuck and tighten it. Drill four straight holes through the end piece and into the bottom. Keep the holes at least ¾ inch away from the sides of the piece to reduce splitting and ⅜ inch above the bottom edge of the end. To do this, you'll have to keep the drill body clear of the work surface.

24. Use the screwdriver to drive a drywall screw snugly into each hole. Be careful not to over-drive the screws so that they tear their way down into the wood; that will weaken rather than strengthen the joint.

25. Repeat steps 22 through 24 to attach the other end piece to the bottom of your toolbox.

26. Slide the sides into position between the end pieces. Drill three holes through the end pieces and into the ends of the side pieces, for a total of twelve holes.

27. Drive a drywall screw into each hole.

28. Turn the toolbox upside down over sawhorses or a corner of your worktable. Drill a row of holes through the bottom piece and into the bottom edge of each side. Then turn over the toolbox and drill a row of holes on the other side of the bottom.

29. Drive a drywall screw through each hole in the bottom.

30. Set the toolbox upright and insert the dowel handle through the holes in the end pieces. Make sure it extends equally beyond the end piece at both ends.

31. Insert the ¼-inch drill bit into your drill so that it is extended to its maximum length (keep at least ½ inch in the drill chuck). Starting at one of the sloped edges of one of the ends, drill through the end and into the center of the dowel. Drill as deep as you can.

32. Keeping the drill running, pull the bit in and out of the hole a couple of times to remove all the sawdust from the hole. Keep the drill aligned in the hole as you're doing this so you don't accidentally make the hole bigger, which will make for a sloppy fit for the dowel.

33. Cut a length of ¼-inch dowel about an inch longer than the drill bit you just used.

34. Spread a little wood glue on a scrap of wood. Roll one end of the dowel in the glue. Insert the glued end into the hole you just drilled and gently hammer the dowel into the hole until it stops traveling.

35. Repeat steps 31 through 34 to pin the handle at the other end of the toolbox.

36. Use a handsaw to cut off the extra dowel pin as close to the surface as possible. Try not to scratch the toolbox with the saw teeth. Use a piece of 100-grit sandpaper wrapped around a block of wood to sand the dowel pin flush with the surface of the wood.

Finishing

37. You are now ready for finishing! Using a paintbrush, apply spar varnish, clear polyurethane, or some other type of weatherproof coating. Paint is not advisable for the inside of your toolbox because the wear and tear of tools would soon do it in.

tongue biting is optional

Horse Sawhorses

Every carpenter needs a good pair of sawhorses. Two horses and a couple of strong planks equal a great work surface; it's portable and can be rearranged to suit all needs. These "horse" sawhorses have an added bonus: They're as suitable for playing with as they are for working on! And if you modify these plans a little bit, you could become the first family on the block to own a pair of saw dogs or saw pigs!

Horse Heads and Rumps

1. From the 1x10, cut two pieces, each about 42 inches long. Each piece will become the body and head of one of the two horses.

2. Starting from one end of each of the two boards you just cut, draw a pencil line about 40 inches long, parallel to and 6¾ inches above the bottom edge of each board. These straight lines will be the "backs" of the horses and the working top edges of the sawhorses.

3. This step will be challenging but fun: Draw a horse's head on the end of each board! Begin the upper part of the horses' necks at the end of the 40-inch line you just drew. The lower part of the horses' necks should end at the bottom of the board. Start with a light outline to get the silhouettes to fit on the available space on the boards, and darken the outlines when you are sure of them. If you'd like a different look — i.e., a saw dog or saw pig — draw the profile that suits your choice.

What You'll Need

TOOLS

Handsaw

Jigsaw

Hammer

Framing square

Speed Square

Block plane

Clamps

Safety glasses

Scissors

MATERIALS

One 8-foot length of 1x10

Two 12-foot lengths of 1x4

One 4-foot length of 1x8

One 10-foot length of 1¾" or wider stock (at least ½ inch thick)

¾"-thick scrap wood

Colorful yarn or raffia, as pictured on the cover

FASTENERS

One pound 4d galvanized box nails

NO TIGHT SPOTS!

Draw your horses' features with smooth lines, avoiding tight inside corners that will be hard to cut out.

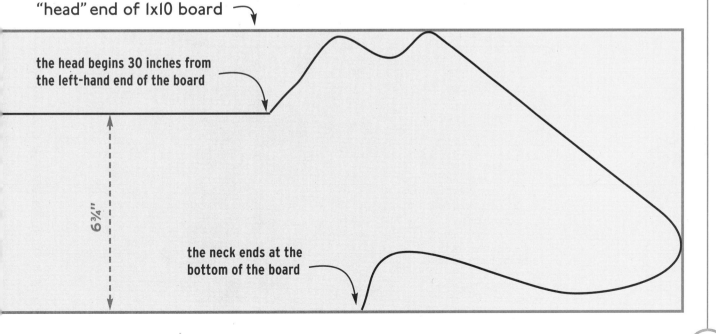

"head" end of 1x10 board

the head begins 30 inches from the left-hand end of the board

6¾"

the neck ends at the bottom of the board

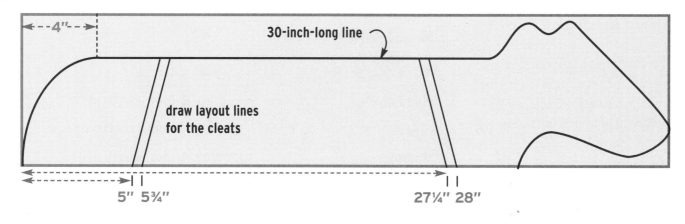

4" ←→

30-inch-long line

draw layout lines
for the cleats

5" 5¾"   27¼" 28"

Camille says: "Electric tools can seem scary and dangerous before you get to know them. The jigsaw seemed like it was just longing to saw off my hand. But trying it for the first time was different from how I thought it was going to be. The jigsaw moved through the wood much faster and more easily than a handsaw. I grew used to its loud sawing noise and constant vibrating.

"It takes time to get to know tools, just like it takes time to get to know people. It's fine if you decide you don't like the jigsaw, but make sure to give it a fair chance, just like you would a new person."

kids!

4. At the opposite end of the boards, draw the downward curve of the horses' rumps starting about 6 inches in from the end of the boards, along that same 40-inch-long pencil line.

5. Now you're ready to mark the location of the cleats that will hold the legs in place when the project is assembled. Stack your two boards with their heads pointing in the same direction. Measuring from the rump end, make layout marks along the bottom edge of one of the pieces at 5, 5¾, 27¼, and 28 inches. Square these lines across the bottom edges of both boards.

6. Using a Speed Square, draw a line at a 15-degree angle from

the four layout marks across each face of the boards. The lines will angle away from the ends of the board, toward the middle. Mark all four board faces this way.

7. Put on your safety glasses, plug in your jigsaw, and use it to carefully cut out the horses' heads, backs, and rumps, following the lines you marked on the boards.

Horse Haunches: The Cleats

8. The cleats are cut from the 1¾-inch stock, and there are a lot of them: eight per sawhorse, or sixteen total. Each cleat is a parallelogram 6¾ inches on both long sides, with 15-degree angles on the ends. Make the first piece as accurately as you can and use it to lay out all the other cuts. It's repetitive work, but the cuts don't have to be perfect. If you are plowing through with a handsaw, you can stack a few pieces, clamp them together, and cut them as a gang.

9. Set the horse bodies on your work surface. Place a cleat along the outside of one of the cleat lines you marked in step 6, with one end flush with the bottom of the board. Nail the cleat on with three box nails, making sure the layout line remains fully visible next to the cleat.

10. Continue placing and nailing on cleats until you have nailed four cleats on each side of each sawhorse body.

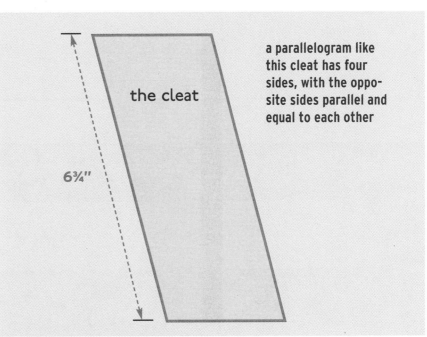

the cleat

6¾"

a parallelogram like this cleat has four sides, with the opposite sides parallel and equal to each other

8

10

¾" slot between cleats

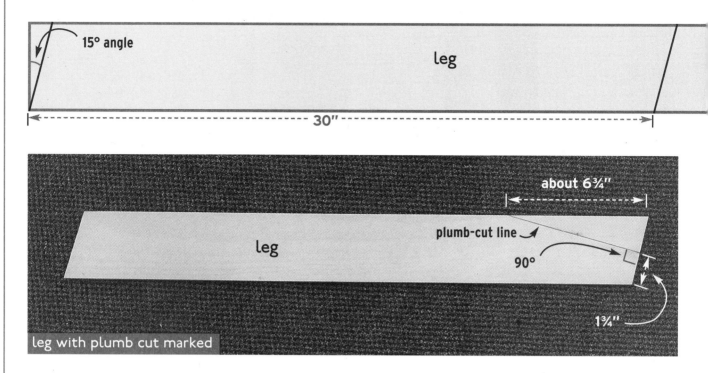

15° angle

leg

30"

about 6¾"

plumb-cut line

90°

1¾"

leg

leg with plumb cut marked

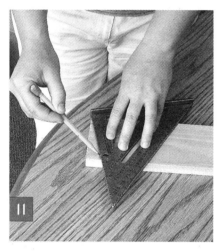

11

14

At Long Last, the Legs

11. Grab your two lengths of 1x4, a pencil, a Speed Square, and a saw. Lay out a 15-degree angle across the end of one of the 1x4 boards. Cut along that line with the saw.

12. From the long point of the cut you just made, measure 30 inches down the board and use that point as the short point of another 15-degree-angled line. Cut along that line with the saw. Your two cuts should be parallel; the finished piece should be a long parallelogram.

13. Each horse needs four legs, of course, for a total of eight. Cut the remaining seven legs now, following the same method you used to cut the first one.

14. The horse legs must be plumb (vertically straight) at the point where they attach to the horse body. To mark a plumb cut on a leg, choose one end of the leg to be the top. Measure 1¾ inches from the short point of that end, along the shorter side of the leg, and mark that point. Using a framing square and starting at the point you just marked, draw a line perpendicular to the end of the leg, extending toward its bottom. This line will run down the leg and should reach the other edge of the board after about 6¾ inches. (See the photo above.)

15. Clamp the board onto a worktable and cut along the plumb-cut line with a saw. Clean up the cut with a couple of passes with your block plane. If the first piece looks accurate, use it as a pattern for tracing cut lines onto the remaining pieces. Cut and plane, cut and plane, until you have completed eight legs.

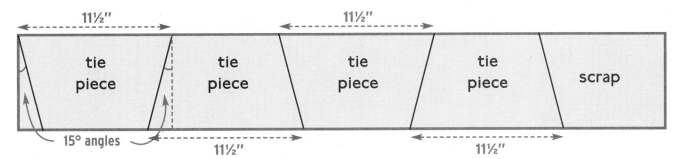

11½"   11½"

tie
piece   tie
piece   tie
piece   tie
piece   scrap

15° angles   11½"   11½"

16. Now you're ready to cut the tie pieces that hold the legs together. On the 1x8 board, draw a 15-degree-angled line across one end. Measure 11½ inches down the board from the long point and draw another 15-degree-angled line *the opposite way* from the first. You will have drawn a trapezoid.

17. Move to the opposite side of the board and measure 11½ inches from the end of the last line that you drew. At that point, draw another line at a 15-degree angle in the opposite direction, so that you make another trapezoid. Repeat this process until you have laid out four of these tie pieces.

18. Cut out all four trapezoids and set them aside.

19. Clear off the worktable. Gather two legs, one tie piece, a piece of ¾-inch-thick scrap wood for a spacer, a handful of box nails, and a hammer. Place the legs with their bottom ends near one edge of the worktable and their plumb cuts facing each other. Place the tie piece on top, so that the assembly is shaped like the letter **A**. Align the top edge of the tie piece 6 inches down from the top of the **A**. Place

the scrap-wood spacer so that its thickness separates the two plumb cuts at the top of the pair of legs. (A spacer that is 6 inches square will both measure and space for you simultaneously.) Check the alignment of all the pieces and adjust them as needed. A couple of clamps may help hold things in place at this stage.

20. Trace around the tie piece with a pencil so that if it shifts position during hammering, you can easily realign it. Drive five or six box nails through one end of

the tie piece and into the leg. Nail the other side the same way, making sure that the spacer can still move freely in the gap between the two legs.

A CAREFUL FIT

Sometimes alignment is everything! As you put together your leg sections, check, double-check, and recheck the position of all the pieces.

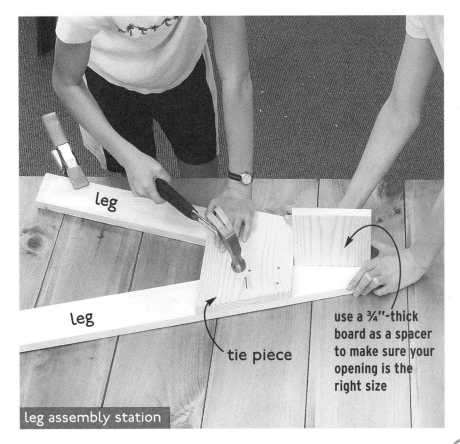

leg

leg

tie piece

use a ¾"-thick board as a spacer to make sure your opening is the right size

leg assembly station

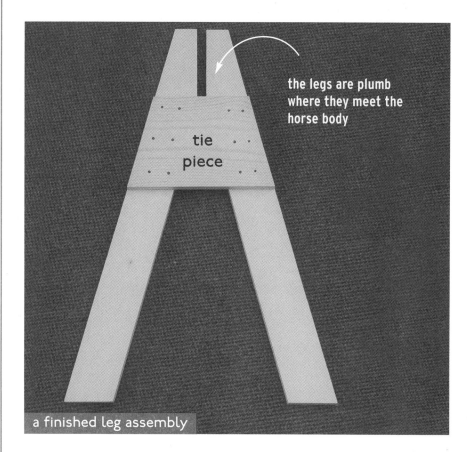

the legs are plumb where they meet the horse body

tie piece

a finished leg assembly

21. Slide your horse body onto the leg assembly. Does it fit? If not, do a little adjusting with a plane, and be sure to take this adjusting into account when you make your next leg assembly.

22. You need to make two complete leg assemblies for each horse … so work hard, work in teams, and take breaks when you need them!

23. When all the leg assemblies are built, put together the horses. If at first they don't slip together easily, don't be dismayed. You need to get the angle between the body and the legs just right, so keep trying!

checking for fit

Now for the Mane and Tail

24. Grab the yarn, a hammer, some box nails, and scissors. To make the mane, hold one arm in front of you with your elbow bent at a right angle and your hand straight up. Grab the loose end of the yarn between your thumb and first finger. With your other hand, make large loops with the yarn, winding it under your elbow and then between your thumb and first finger, over and over again, keeping it fairly taut. Continue until you have made about twenty or so loops.

25. Carefully remove the yarn from your arm and lay it evenly across the neck of your horse. The yarn should naturally fall in two bunches, one from each side of the loop. Use a pair of scissors to snip both ends of the yarn loops.

26. Hammer a nail about one third of the way into the edge of the horse's neck just above one bunch. Then use the hammer to bend the rest of the nail down over the yarn to hold it in place. Hammer another nail down in the same manner to secure the other bunch of yarn.

27. If you want a thicker mane, you can make another set of loops, creating four bunches of yarn instead of two.

28. Make the tail the same way as the mane: Wrap the yarn from elbow to fingers about forty times. This time, when you remove the yarn from your arm, simply snip all the yarn at one end of the loop, creating forty nice long pieces of yarn. Tie all these pieces together with a small piece of yarn about 1 inch from the end.

29. Hold the tail against the rear of a horse, where a tail should be. Split the yarn into two groups, left and right. Hammer a nail about one third of the way into the board, between and just below the groups of yarn. As you did to secure the mane, bend the rest of the nail up to hold the yarn in place. Now braid it, brush it, or put in a ribbon!

30. Repeat the mane- and tail-making processes for the second sawhorse.

31. Painting is optional, but painted eyes are a nice touch, as are ears made of cardboard or another stiff material. Just remember that these are work animals — don't make them so beautiful that you won't want to use them for future carpentry projects (or a ride around the yard)!

bend the nail to hold the yarn

flip it

This is a game that Barbara played (and loved) at school as a child, and it is now one of Camille and Allegra's favorite games. It's a simple but compelling game that includes moving parts, quick action, and math. Making your own set is a challenge, but it will be well worth the effort.

What You'll Need

TOOLS

Handsaw

Finish saw

Hacksaw

Ruler, combination square,
  or framing square

Drill

$\frac{9}{64}$-inch drill bit

$\frac{1}{8}$-inch drill bit

Hammer

Nail set

Awl

Metal file

Scissors

Sanding block

Block plane

Clamps

Safety glasses

MATERIALS

One 4-foot length of $1\frac{5}{16}$-
  inch L-shaped outside
  corner bead molding

One small piece of $\frac{1}{4}$-inch
  plywood, 10 inches
  x 10 inches or larger

One 3-foot length of $\frac{1}{8}$-inch
  brass or steel rod

One 4-foot length of $\frac{1}{2}$-inch
  x $\frac{3}{4}$-inch parting bead

Fourteen $\frac{1}{8}$-inch steel or
  brass washers

One sheet of 120-grit
  sandpaper

Carpenter's glue

Fine-point indelible pen

Colored highlighter or marking pens

Felt (approximately
  10 inches x 10 inches)

Two short lengths of scrap
  wood

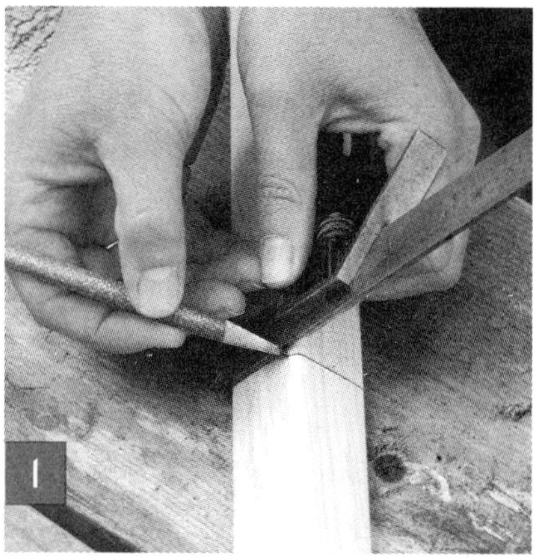

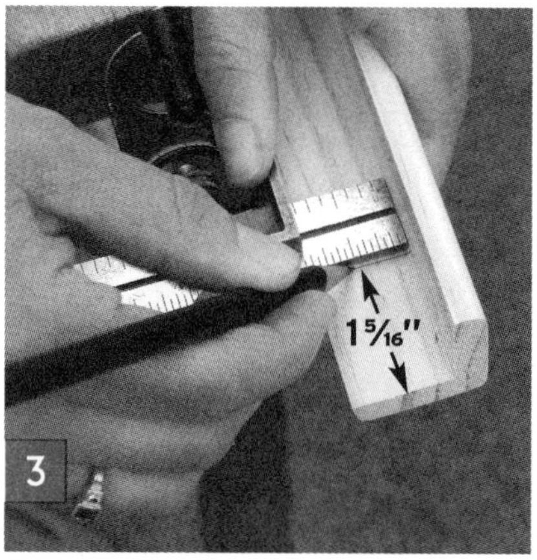

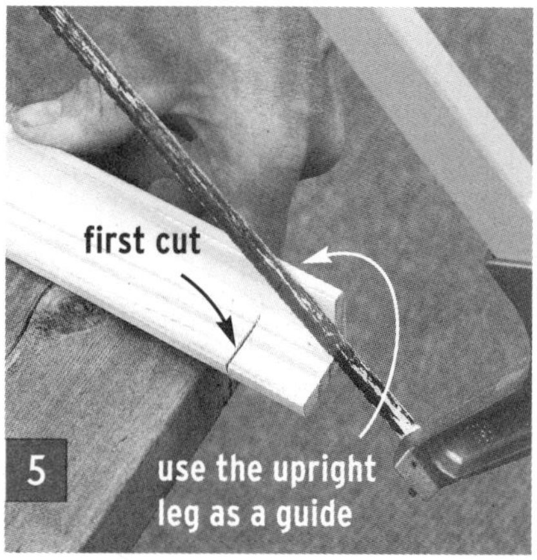

Cutting and Assembling the Frame

1. Place the L-shaped corner bead molding on the work surface with its outside corner facing up. Square lines along both faces at 10 inches and 20 inches from one end. Use a finish saw or hacksaw to make straight cuts through the molding at each line. The two 10-inch pieces you cut will be the sides of the gameboard frame.

2. From the remaining corner bead molding, measure, mark, and cut two 9⅛-inch lengths for the top and bottom of the frame.

to parents

A utility knife is the best tool for trimming the joints to make them tight, but using the knife in this way leaves open the possibility of blade meeting fingers. If your kids are having trouble with the joint, you may want to step in and use a utility knife to fine-tune the cut.

These two pieces should have smooth, flat ends so that you will be able to make tight, strong glue joints, so take out any roughness on the ends with sandpaper and a sanding block.

3. Clamp one of the 10-inch lengths of molding to the edge of the work surface, with one leg of the molding upright, so that the piece extends a couple of inches past the edge. Square a line 1⁵⁄₁₆ inches in from the end across the bottom leg of the molding.

4. Use your finish saw or hacksaw to cut along the line you marked. Stop the cut when you reach the inside of the upright leg.

5. Lay the saw blade against the inside of the upright leg, using it for a guide, and rip through the base leg until you intersect the first cut. Remove the piece you've cut out.

6. Assemble the corner as shown in the photo at right to check the fit. If the corner joint is not tight, you can adjust it by cutting away more with the saw or by sanding.

7. Unclamp the notched piece and rotate it so that the opposite end extends past the edge of your work surface, with the same leg upright as before. Clamp it down and repeat the measuring, marking, cutting, and sanding of steps 3 through 6. When you finish, one leg of the L-shaped molding should be notched on both ends.

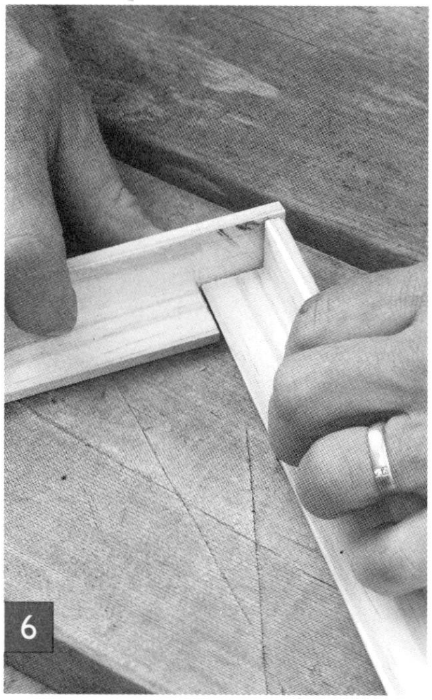

8. Make the same notch cuts on both ends of the other 10-inch piece of corner molding. Then test-assemble the game-board frame as shown in the photo at right. If any of the corner joints don't fit tightly, sand down bumpy, irregular, or uneven spots until they do.

Cutting Out the Bottom and the Felt

9. Bring the plywood to your work surface and orient it so that the grain runs left to right. With a framing square or combination square, mark two points 9 inches apart along the top edge of the plywood. Square two lines down from these points. On each line, mark a point 9⅛ inches from the top edge. Draw a line connecting these marks to complete the layout of the bottom piece.

10. Use a finish saw to cut along all three lines. Make the two crosscuts (longer lines) first and then the rip cut. The piece you cut out will be the bottom of the game board. Place it inside your frame pieces to check the fit, and trim it if necessary. A small gap around the perimeter is ideal.

11. Use the plywood bottom piece as a pattern to make the felt covering. Place the plywood bottom on the felt and trace around it. Cut the felt about ⅛ inch bigger all around than the pattern you traced; the felt should be a bit larger than the plywood bottom.

game-board test assembly

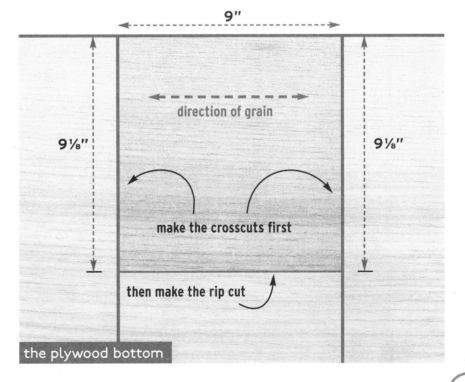

9"

direction of grain

9⅛"

9⅛"

make the crosscuts first

then make the rip cut

the plywood bottom

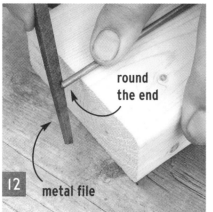

round the end

metal file

12

scrap wood

clamp at a right angle

14

16

Cutting the Metal Rods

12. Measure and mark two 9¾-inch lengths on the metal rod. Cut the rod at these points with a hacksaw. Round the sharp edges with a few passes of a file or sandpaper.

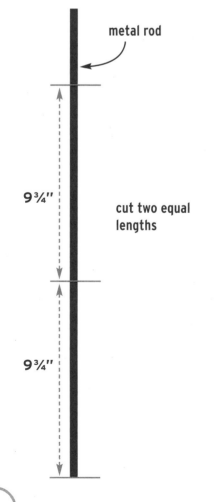

metal rod

9¾"

cut two equal lengths

9¾"

Putting the Game Board Together

13. Clear off your work surface and gather a couple of short lengths of scrap wood, two clamps, the carpenter's glue, and the game-board frame pieces and bottom.

14. Clamp one of the scrap pieces at a right angle to the near edge of your work surface. Use a square to align the scrap block accurately, as the rest of the assembly depends upon precise right angles!

15. Set one of the notched frame side pieces against the scrap block. Position the unnotched top and bottom pieces in the two notches and make sure the nearer one is parallel with the edge of the table. Place the other notched side piece in position. (The frame should look just as it did in step 8; see page 85.) Check to see that the frame looks square. Now is the time for any final adjustments to make the joints fit tightly.

16. Take note of how the end surfaces of the unnotched moldings meet the notched moldings. Pick up one of the unnotched pieces and spread a little bit of carpenter's glue on the L-shaped surfaces at both ends of the piece. Replace the piece and slide it into the notches so that the glue makes contact on both ends.

17. Lift up the other unnotched piece, spread glue on both of its ends, and slide it into place.

18. Check that the closer unnotched side is still parallel to the table edge. Clamp the second block of scrap wood very loosely just next to the free side of the assembled frame. Slide the block gently against the frame to put a little pressure on the glue joints, making sure not to distort them. This might require a couple of tries, and it's easiest with one person working the clamp and another adjusting the block. When the block is pressed up against the frame and the frame looks just right, tighten the clamp.

the game-board frame is sandwiched between the scrap-wood blocks

tightening the clamps

SQUARE AND MORE SQUARE

Keeping it square is the name of the game. As you're assembling and gluing the frame, check and recheck to make sure that you have right angles at all of your corners.

20

21

19. Carefully check to see that the plywood bottom will fit into the assembled frame, and trim it with sandpaper or a block plane if it doesn't. There should be a small gap around the perimeter of the plywood bottom inside the game-board frame, which the felt will cover when your game board is finished.

20. Place the plywood bottom on your work surface with its better side facing up. Squeeze a thin line of carpenter's glue around the perimeter of the bottom, about ⅜ inch in from the edge. Spread out the glue with a fingertip or a scrap of wood, working it toward the outside edge.

21. Turn over the bottom piece and set it gently inside the frame. Find something heavy that fits inside the frame to weight down the bottom piece while the glue sets. Let the glue harden for an hour or more before moving the frame. Meanwhile, there is more work to do!

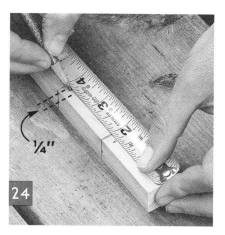

Making the Flip Keys

22. Place the length of parting bead on your work surface so that one of its wider faces is up. Starting from one end, make a mark every 2 inches until you have laid out fifteen small pieces. These will become the flip keys for the game. (Only twelve flip keys are needed, but making extra will allow you to discard a few if they don't turn out perfectly.)

to parents

If your kids are way off the mark when drilling through the keys, try this technique: Have them drill halfway through, then turn the piece over and drill the rest of the way through from the other side. This way, if they're not drilling perfectly straight, they'll be working with only half the distance at a time and won't have as much opportunity to veer off course. If they can't make the two holes meet up, have them turn over the piece once more and drill again from the first side.

23. With a framing square, draw lines across the face of the parting bead at each point you marked. Then extend the lines around to both of the narrow sides, so that the lines are marked on three of the four sides.

24. Set the parting bead on edge with the same end you measured from in step 22 on the right. Measuring from this end, mark the center of the short face (roughly ¼ inch in from either edge) at a point ¼ inch to the right of each of the lines. Your first mark should be at 1¾ inches, the second at 3¾ inches, and so on. This is where you will drill through the keys later.

25. Turn over the piece and mark the drilling centers the same way on the other short face.

26. Use an awl or a nail tip to make a small indentation at each of the drilling points.

27. Clamp the marked parting bead on top of a piece of scrap wood. Put the %4-inch bit in the drill chuck.

28. You are going to drill straight through each marked key, with the drill bit starting at one of the indentations and coming out at the matching one on the other side. Start by drilling the first piece all the way through. Unclamp the parting bead and see how well you did. If the hole is not quite perfect, you can drill back from the exit side to correct small inaccuracies. Notice the direction of the error and try to correct your aim when you drill the next key.

29. After you have drilled all the holes, use a handsaw to cut each flip key from the parting bead. Keep it clamped on edge and saw along the layout lines.

Use the lines on the wide face of the board as guides to help keep the cut square.

Finishing Touches

30. Using the 120-grit sandpaper and a sanding block, sand all surfaces of the keys, including the corners, until they are smooth. This might seem a little time consuming, but the smooth feel of the keys is part of the enjoyment of playing the game.

31. Color twelve of the flip keys, on both sides and on the edges, too. The quickest way we found to color the keys is with highlighter pens. If you would prefer to stain the keys, you can, but do not paint them. If you want alternating colors on your board, do half the keys in one color and the other half in another color.

32. Making sure the drilled holes are at the top of the keys, use an indelible fine-point pen to number the flip keys 1 through 12, marking one number on each key. Number just

numbering the flip keys

one side of each key. Make your numbers big and bold.

33. Bring the game-board frame to your work surface and look it over. If the ends of the sides are not perfectly flush with the top and bottom moldings, gently run the sanding block, with sandpaper, along the length of the tops and bottoms of the moldings until the ends are flush. Take your time. Pushing too hard might cause the glue joints to break open.

34. Move to the tops and bottoms of the corners and sand them until they follow the curve of the molding where the joints come together. Again, work gently and patiently.

the corner before sanding

the corner after sanding

to parents

The metal rods should fit tightly in the drilled holes. However, if they develop a tendency to loosen up and fall out, the recess can be filled with epoxy or another strong glue to hold them in place.

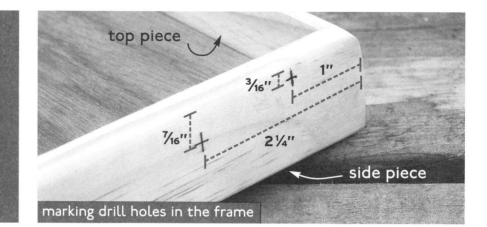

top piece

³/₁₆" · 1"

⁷/₁₆" · 2¼"

side piece

marking drill holes in the frame

35. Choose one of the short (unnotched) sides of the frame to be the top of the game board. On the outside of one side piece, lightly square a line 1 inch down from the top. On that line, mark a point ³/₁₆ inch down from the upper edge of the side. Use an awl to set the mark into the wood. Repeat this process on the opposite upper corner of the frame.

36. On one side piece, lightly square a line 2¼ inches down from the top. On that line, mark a point ⁷/₁₆ inch down from the upper edge of the side. Use an awl to set the mark. Repeat the process on the upper corner of the opposite side.

37. Put the ⅛-inch bit in the drill chuck. Drill through the sides of the frame at the four points you just marked. Try to keep the holes as straight as possible. Alignment is crucial!

38. Spread a thin, even layer of glue along the surface of the bottom piece. Gently lay the piece of felt over the glue, edging the bottom corners into place first and then smoothing the felt to the top with your fingers.

Stringing and Placing the Flip Keys

39. Gather the metal rods, the flip keys, and the washers. Push the first rod through one of

the lower holes, across the game board, and into the drilled hole on the opposite side. Use the nail set and hammer to tap it into final position. This rod will be the key rest. It should be recessed slightly from the surface of the frame on both sides.

40. Slide the second rod a little way through the upper hole on the right-hand side and begin stringing on the keys. Begin with a washer, then the number 12 key, and then a washer. Slide the rest of the keys onto the rod in numerical order, with a washer between each pair. End with a washer. Then set the end of the rod in the final remaining hole and tap it into position with the nail set.

38

39

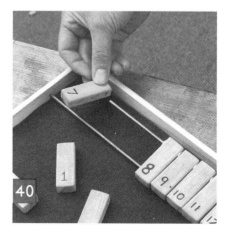

40

camille's directions for playing flip it

Flip It can be played by any number of people. The winner is the lucky player who has the lowest score. Have fun!

1. To set up the game, put all keys in the down position.

2. Roll two dice out onto the felt.

3. Find the sum of the numbers rolled.

4. Flip up the key marked with this sum, or flip up two or more keys whose numbers together add up to the amount rolled. For example: If you roll a 3 and a 4, you can choose to put up the 7, the 6 and 1, the 5 and 2, or the 3 and 4.

5. Continue rolling and flipping up keys until you are unable to flip up keys for the number rolled. (Once a key has been flipped up, it cannot be put down or used again.)

6. Add up the numbers on the keys still down. The total is your score. Try to get the lowest score you can!

allegra's table

W hen we asked Allegra to describe the table of her dreams, she knew just what to say. It would be a table built for drawing pictures on, it would be small enough to fit in her room, and it would be just the right height to work on while sitting on her Sturdy Stool (see page 56). You can vary the dimensions to make your own dream table. These basic plans can be used to make anything from a card table to a low Japanese-style table. The dimensions given will produce an 18½-inch by 32-inch table tall enough to accommodate a child's chair.

We recommend that you put a clear finish on your table. Polyurethane varnish is a good choice. It comes in either an oil-based or a water-based formulation. The oil-based finish will impart a rich golden hue to most woods, while the water-based finish will yield a clearer, less modified look.

What You'll Need

TOOLS

Jigsaw or handsaw

Tape measure

Hammer

Combination square or Speed Square

Framing square

Drill

⅛-inch drill bit

⅜-inch or ½-inch Forstner bit (same size as wood plugs)

Phillips-head screwdriver

Block plane

Two or three bar clamps about 24 inches long

Safety glasses

MATERIALS

One 6-foot length of ⁵⁄₄×10 clear or #2 pine board

One 8-foot length of ⁵⁄₄×4 clear or #2 pine board

Four 36-inch square pine or cedar balusters

⅜-inch or ½-inch wood plugs or buttons

Carpenter's wood glue

120-grit sandpaper

150-grit sandpaper

Polyurethane varnish (or finish coat of your choice)

Paintbrush

Wax paper or newspaper

Rags

FASTENERS

Four 1½-inch corner irons and matching screws

A handful of 2-inch drywall screws

combination square

Making the Tabletop

1. Cut the 6-foot length of ⅝×10 board in half by measuring 36 inches in from either end, squaring a line across, and cutting along the line. The cut edges will be trimmed off later, so this rough cut does not need to be made perfectly.

2. Place the two pieces you just cut side by side on a flat work surface, with their most attractive surfaces facing up. Check the joint between the boards to make sure there aren't any gaps. Try turning the boards over or flipping them end to end until you have the tightest possible joint between them.

3. Position two bar clamps about 8 inches in from each end of the tabletop and adjust them so you can clamp the boards together. Tighten the clamps and then look closely at the joint, which should be nearly invisible. If it is, you are ready to glue. If it's not, try tightening the clamps a little more. You can also reposition the clamps or use more clamps. Glue will fill small cracks between the boards, but it's best if the joint is nice and tight.

small bar clamp

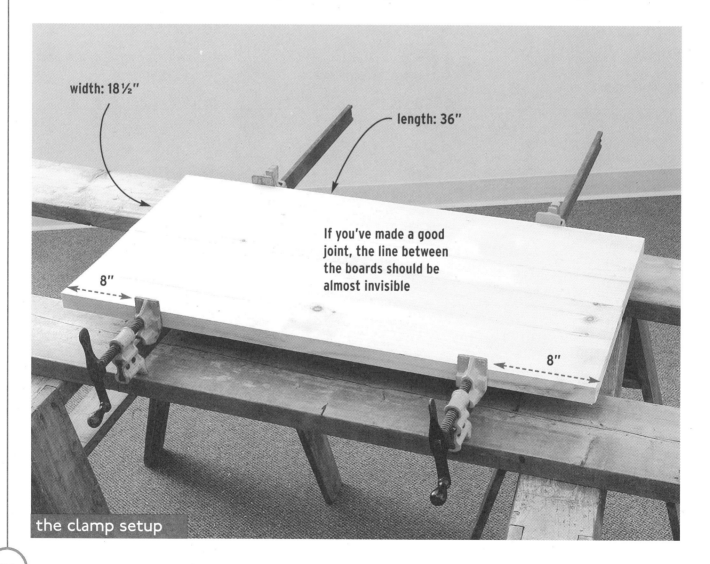

width: 18½"

length: 36"

If you've made a good joint, the line between the boards should be almost invisible

8"

8"

the clamp setup

5

7

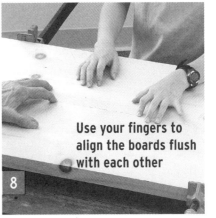

Use your fingers to align the boards flush with each other

8

The Great Glue-Up

4. Spread a length of wax paper or newspaper beneath the joint in the tabletop to protect your work surface, since glue will ooze out of the joint as the clamping pressure increases. Place a damp rag nearby for wiping away excess glue and cleaning fingers. Loosen the clamps and put them where they can be repositioned easily. Once the glue is spread, you won't have much time before it begins to set, so you'll want to have everything close at hand.

5. Making sure not to change the orientation of the boards, tilt the nearer one on edge and spread glue on the surface where it will be joined.

6. Use a scrap of wood, a piece of cardboard, or your finger to work the glue into a thin, even layer along the length of the board. Too much glue will make the pieces slide out of alignment when you clamp them; with too little, your glue joint may not bond well and could come apart later.

7. Realign the two tabletop pieces and position the clamps in the same spots they were in for the dry run. Tighten each clamp only enough to keep it in place. A little glue may ooze out of the joint at this point.

8. After all the clamps are in position, check that the ends of the boards are even and the top surfaces of the boards are flush. If they're not, push down on the higher one until they are. Loosen the nearest clamp if you need to, but be sure to tighten it gently once the boards are back in proper position.

9. When the joint looks good, tighten the clamps evenly all around. An even row of tiny beads of glue squeezed out of the joint is a sure sign of success; it indicates that you spread enough glue to make a sound glue joint. Wipe away the excess glue with a damp rag.

10. Leave the tabletop undisturbed in the clamps for at least two hours; the longer the drying period, the better.

to parents

If every cut and joint were made with absolute precision, this little table would never rock, jiggle, or tip. But with kids wielding all the tools, the result will have more personality . . . that is, it probably will end up with a few little imperfections. Plane and sand liberally, and appreciate the artistry of your own handmade furniture.

Wipe away the excess glue with a damp rag

9

The Four-Piece Apron

11. Bring your ¾×4 board to your work surface. If you are using a jigsaw, set it to cut at a 45-degree angle. If you are using a handsaw, reread the instructions for making a bevel cut on pages 14–15.

12. Square a line across the board a couple of inches away from the right-hand end. From the ends of this line, mark a 45-degree angle on both edges of the board. Then make the cut. The board will now have a bevel cut on one end.

13. Hook your tape measure on the long point of the end with the bevel cut, measure 28 inches down the board, and square a line across at that point. Clamp the board to the work surface so that the marked portion hangs over the right-hand edge. From this line, mark a 45-degree angle on the edges of the board, with the long point of this cut on the same side of the

board as the long point of the cut you made in the previous step. Then make the cut (you probably will have to walk around to the other side of the board to align the saw blade properly). The piece you cut off will be one of the long sides of the apron.

14. Turn over the remaining part of the board so that its long point is on top. Repeat step 13 to cut a matching long apron piece.

15. Again, turn over the remainder of the board so that the long point of the bevel cut is on top. Measure 14½ inches down the board from the long point and square a line there. Mark a 45-degree angle on the edges of the board, with the long point of this cut on the same side of the board as the existing long point. Then make the cut to free one of the short apron ends from the board.

16. Repeat step 15 to make the other short apron end.

The Legs

17. Bring the balusters to your work surface. We used square cedar porch-rail balusters, but if you want a fancier table, you could make your legs from turned stair balusters. To fit the table to the seat of your choice, the legs should be 10 to 12 inches taller than the top of the seat. We cut our balusters to 20 inches. Square a line across each baluster at the appropriate measurement and make a square (90-degree) cut there.

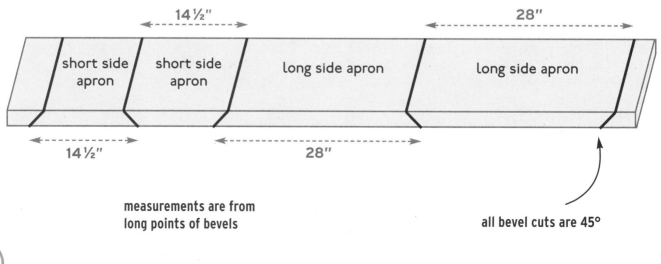

14½"   14½"   28"   28"

short side apron | short side apron | long side apron | long side apron

measurements are from long points of bevels

all bevel cuts are 45°

Drilling the Apron and the Legs

18. Lay one of the short sides of the apron flat on your work surface with its two long points on top. Square a line across the face of the piece ¾ inch in from one end. Mark two points along this line, ¾ inch in from each side of the board. Repeat this process at the opposite end of the board.

19. Measure and mark the other short side the same way.

20. Fit the Forstner bit in the drill chuck. Drill a hole about as deep as your plugs (usually ⅜ inch or so) at each of the eight points you marked.

21. Lay one of the legs on your work surface. On one side, mark a point ¾ inch down from the top, in the center of the leg, with a generous X. Turn the leg so that an adjacent side faces up;

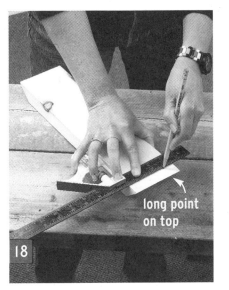

long point on top

mark a point 2¾ inches down from the top, in the center, with another X.

22. Measure and mark the other three legs the same way.

23. Put the ⅛-inch drill bit in the drill chuck and bore a pilot hole through the legs at each of the points you marked. You can use a countersink bit if you want the leg to look very tidy under the table.

Allegra says: "Making a bevel cut is hard. When I made them for this table, I had to keep checking to make sure I was cutting on the lines. This was the most complicated part of building the table. The funnest part was putting in the plugs at the end. It was so simple and it made the table look great! But overall, the whole table was fun, even if it was hard."

kids!

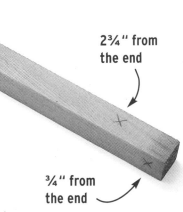

the pilot holes are on adjacent sides of the leg

2¾" from the end

¾" from the end

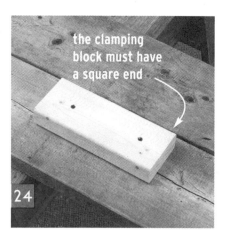

the clamping block must have a square end

24

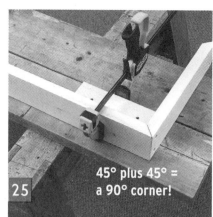

45° plus 45° = a 90° corner!

25

26

Apron Assembly

24. Fastening together a mitered joint is easier when you have a clamping block to fasten the pieces to while you set your screws. Find a piece of scrap wood (a 2x4 piece will work well) with a square end. Screw or clamp it down to your work surface near one of the corners, leaving enough room that you can lay one of the apron pieces outside of the clamping block and have it still rest on the table.

25. Set one of the long apron pieces on edge against the longer side of the clamping block, aligning the inside of one of its mitered ends with the corner of the block. Clamp the apron piece in place. Then set one of the short ends of the apron against the adjacent side of the clamping block, fitting the two angled ends together to make the mitered corner.

26. Holding the short side in place, drill a ⅛-inch pilot hole through the center of one of the predrilled Forstner holes into the

end of the long apron piece. Then drive a 2-inch drywall screw into this hole to fasten the corner together. Check the alignment of the miter joint; you can loosen the screw and adjust the joint if necessary. When you're satisfied with the joint, drill a pilot hole and drive a screw into the other predrilled Forstner

hole. Tighten both screws to complete the corner.

27. Continue clamping, drilling, and screwing together the rest of the joints until you have a completed rectangular apron. You may have to reposition your clamping block in order to work all of the joints.

screws are driven through the short pieces into the long pieces

the finished apron

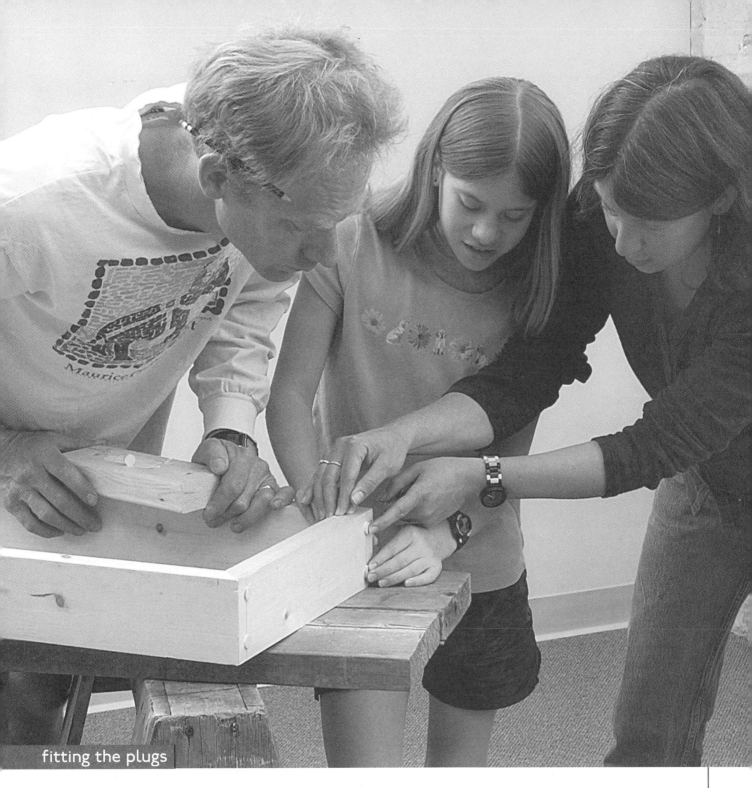

fitting the plugs

Glue and Plug

28. Spread a thin layer of wood glue on a small scrap of wood. If you are using wood plugs, turn one of the plugs on edge and roll it in the glue. Fit the plug into one of the holes in the apron. Place a little block of wood over the plug and hammer the wood. The block ensures that the plug doesn't get driven too far into the hole. If you are using buttons, use a sliver of wood to put a little glue on the sidewalls of one of the holes in the apron and then fit the button into the hole. Tap it gently into place with a hammer.

29. Keep gluing and plugging until all the holes are filled. If you've used plugs, after the glue is set you can either sand the plugs flush with the rest of the apron — the usual way of treating them — or leave them standing out or *proud*, as a carpenter would say.

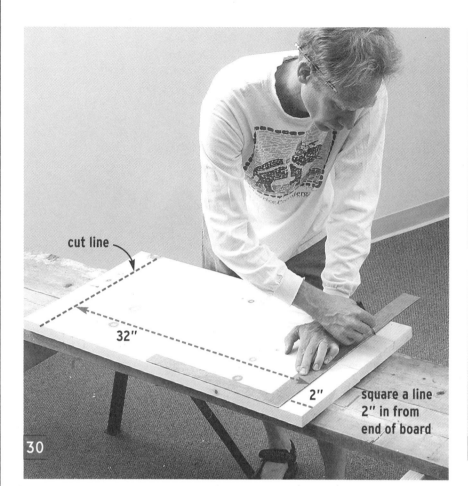

cut line

32"

2"

square a line
2" in from
end of board

30

31

32

Putting It All Together

30. Now you're ready to trim the tabletop to its finished length. Square a line across the width of the tabletop about 2 inches in from one end. From this line, measure 32 inches

GLUE, THEN CUT

It's best to make a "glue-up" (a piece that you've glued together) extra long and cut it to size later because it's almost impossible to line up the piece's ends perfectly before the glue starts to set. Never cut to size before the glue is completely dry!

across the face of the table and square another line across there. Cut along both of these lines.

31. Sand the entire surface of the tabletop with 120-grit sandpaper. The end grain on the edges is hard to sand, but the result is worth it! Then go over the top again with 150-grit sandpaper.

32. Mount a corner iron on the interior end of one of the long sides of the apron, close to the outside corner. Set the top flange (arm) of the iron slightly below the top edge of the long side so that the tabletop can be pulled down tight to the apron. Fasten the corner iron in place with the screws that came with it.

33. Mount a corner iron to the other end of the same long apron piece. Then mount a corner iron at each end of the other long apron piece.

34. Turn over the table apron so that the top flanges of the corner irons face the work surface. Stand a table leg upside down (with its top resting on the work surface) inside one of the apron corners. Rotate the leg until both of the layout Xs are visible on the inside of the apron frame. Then slip a coin or a thin, flat scrap of wood underneath the leg to serve as a spacer. Drive a 2-inch drywall screw through each pilot hole and into the table apron to secure the table leg.

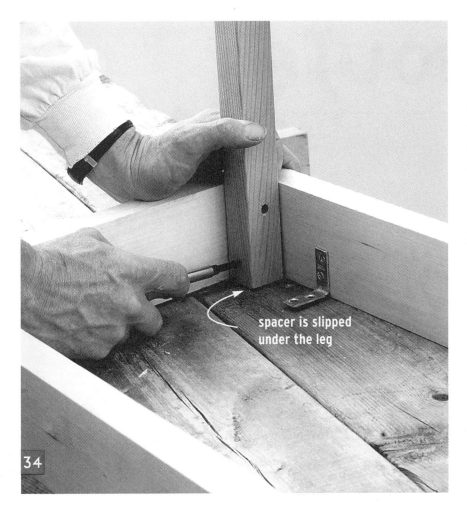

spacer is slipped under the leg

34

36

35. Fasten the remaining three legs to the apron in the same way.

36. Turn the tabletop face-down on a smooth surface that won't scratch or mar the pine, such as a clean piece of plywood or an old towel. Turn the assembled apron and legs upside down and place them on top of it. Adjust the leg-and-apron assembly until the tabletop has an even 2-inch overhang on all sides of the apron. Fasten the corner irons to the tabletop with the screws that came with them.

Finishing

37. Sand the table with 120-grit paper. Brush away all the dust, then apply a coat of polyurethane varnish.

38. After the first coat has dried, sand the table lightly with 150-grit paper, then apply a second coat of polyurethane.

> ### FINISH COATS
>
> Always put the same number of finish coats on all sides (the top, the bottom, and the edges) of wood projects. Otherwise, the wood can absorb more moisture through the uncoated surfaces, which could cause it to warp.

book House

This project has it all: sawing, nailing, drilling, and shingling. It's also an opportunity to be creative and to make something useful at the same time. We have mapped out the steps for making a house-shaped bookcase, complete with an upstairs, a downstairs, and an attic for arranging smaller books, furniture, or a family of stuffed animals. You can add a swinging front door, moldings, and miniature windows if you want to really make your Book House a home.

What You'll Need

TOOLS

Handsaw or jigsaw

Phillips-head screwdriver

Flat-head screwdriver (if needed for the hinges)

Hammer

Framing square

Speed Square

Drill

⅛-inch drill bit

¹⁄₁₆-inch drill bit

Nail set

Awl

Clamps

Safety glasses

MATERIALS

One 4-foot by 8-foot sheet of ¼-inch luaun plywood

One 14-foot length of 1x10 (cut to 10'6" and 3'6" if necessary for transport)

One 4-foot length of 1x12

One 2-foot length of 1¾-inch lattice or panel stock (about ⅜ inch thick)

Short (10¾-inch) length of 1x6 board (optional)

One bundle 15-inch white cedar shingles

FASTENERS

One pound 8d stainless or galvanized ring-shank siding nails

One packet 1-inch white paneling nails

Four 1¼-inch drywall screws

One pair small (1½ inches by 2 inches) hinges, with screws

to parents

When you look at the instructions, you will see that two 45-degree bevel cuts are called for on the shelf sides. To simplify things, we advise letting an adult make these cuts. They can be done with a circular saw or a jigsaw set to the correct angle. Laying out and cutting the plywood back is likely to be less interesting to kids, so again parents might want to step in and get it done ahead of time.

The gang we worked with all had a good time making the straight cuts with the handsaw and clamped-on guide. They made less-than-perfect joints on the shelves, but the fun they had making them more than filled in those tiny gaps.

Marking and Cutting the Back Piece

1. Place the sheet of plywood on your work surface. Square a line 24 inches from one end across the width of the sheet. Use a saw to crosscut the sheet along that line.

2. Draw a line lengthwise down the center of the 24-inch-wide piece, 12 inches from either edge. On the centerline, mark a point 37½ inches down from one end of the piece. From that same end, mark a point 25½ inches down on both edges. Draw lines connecting the marks on the sides to the mark on the centerline. These lines trace the peaked roof of the back piece. Cut along the layout lines with a saw, and set the back piece aside.

Marking and Cutting the Sides and Shelves

3. Bring the 1x10 (the longer portion of the board, if you had to cut it to get it home from the lumberyard) to your work surface. Square a line 26 inches in from one end of the board. This is the long point of the bevel cut you are going to make. Using your Speed Square, draw a line from this point at a 45-degree angle on the edge of the board, angling back toward the end of the board you measured from.

4. If you're working with a handsaw, reread the instructions for making a bevel cut on pages 14–15. If you're working with a jigsaw, set the saw to cut at a 45-degree angle. Take a good look at the jigsaw blade to make sure it is going to cut the angle you have drawn. Check and recheck your reference line! Then cut straight across the board. You have just cut out the first side piece.

5. Take a look at the beveled edge of the remaining part of the board. If it is very irregular, you might need to make a new bevel cut; turn your board over, square a line, and make a new cut across it. Once you have a good clean beveled edge, you're ready to cut the other side piece. If you're using a jigsaw, reset the saw to cut at 90 degrees. Square a line 26 inches from the long point of the beveled edge and make the cut at a 90-degree angle. Set both side pieces aside.

6. Cut three 22½-inch lengths from the remaining 1x10. These pieces will be the bottom, middle, and top shelves. Keep the shelves together as a group and set them aside.

Cutting the Roof Parts

7. Because the roof joint is lapped, the two roof pieces are different lengths — something you'll need to remember when assembly time comes. Bring the 4-foot length of 1x12 to your work surface. Draw a line down its length 10¼ inches in from one side and then use a saw to rip the board along that line.

8. Crosscut the ripped board into two pieces, one 20¼ inches long and the other 21 inches long. The rest of the board is scrap.

9. Clamp the lattice or panel stock to your work surface so that about 12 inches hangs over the edge. Square lines across it 10½ and 21 inches from one end. Use your saw to make cuts at both these marks. The two 10½-inch pieces you cut free are the ridge boards that will be fastened to the roof at its peak. Set the ridge boards aside with the other roof parts.

Cutting the Cubby Sides and the Door

10. Bring the remaining length of 1x10 to your work surface. Draw a line down its length 8¼ inches in from one side and then rip the board along that line.

11. Crosscut the ripped board into two pieces, each 11 inches long. These will be the sides of the cubby (the front entrance hall of your Book House), and their front edges will be concealed by the door.

12. The door is a simple rectangle 10¾ inches long and 5½ inches wide. If you have on hand a short piece of 1x6 board (which, of course, is 5½ inches wide), you can cut the door from it. Otherwise, cut your door to size from the remaining 1x10 board.

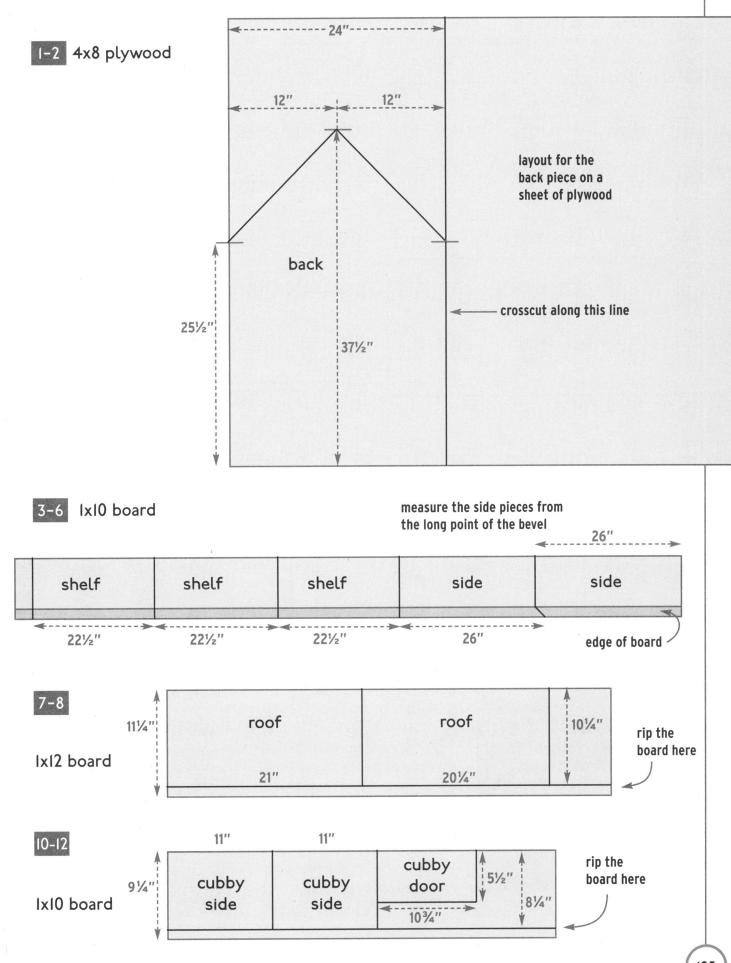

1–2 4x8 plywood

24"

12" 12"

back

layout for the
back piece on a
sheet of plywood

25½"

37½"

crosscut along this line

3–6 1x10 board

measure the side pieces from
the long point of the bevel

26"

| shelf | shelf | shelf | side | side |

22½" 22½" 22½" 26"

edge of board

7–8

1x12 board

11¼"

roof   roof   10¼"

21"   20¼"

rip the
board here

10–12

1x10 board

9¼"

11"   11"

cubby
side   cubby
side   cubby
door   5½"

8¼"

10¾"

rip the
board here

Mark up two identical shelves.
Only two of the shelves are marked up with lines and Xs. The third shelf remains blank.

Mark up two identical sides.

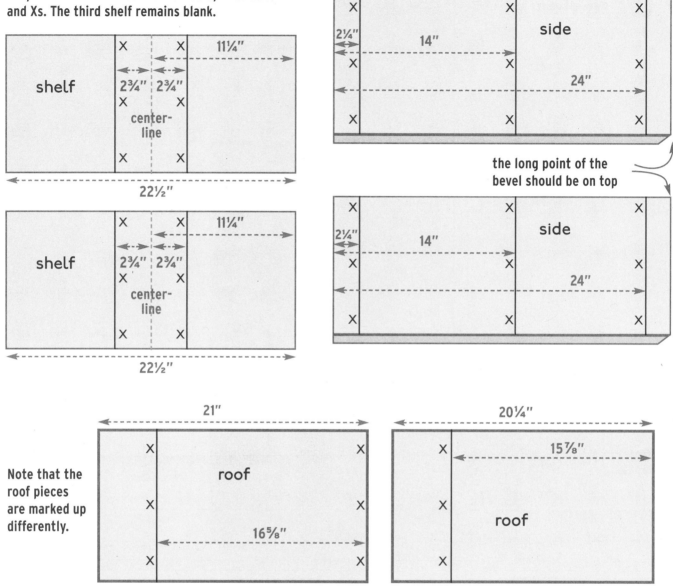

the long point of the bevel should be on top

Note that the roof pieces are marked up differently.

Marking the Assembly Layout

13. Measure and draw layout lines and Xs on the pieces you've cut as shown in the illustrations above. Pay close attention to where to put the Xs when you are drawing these lines. The Xs will be covered by other parts during assembly. A visible X in a completed piece means that something is amiss!

Cubby Assembly

14. Bring the cubby sides and the two shelves that have been marked with lines to your worktable. Turn one of the shelves so that the lined side faces down and start an 8d nail opposite each of the six Xs, driving them most of the way through the board.

15. Stand the cubby side pieces upright and parallel to

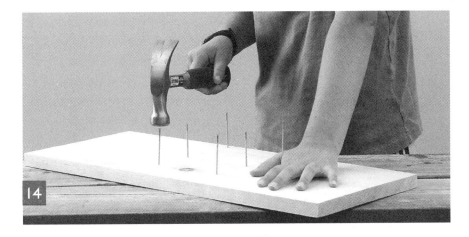
14

of three nails will support one end of a shelf.

19. Choose the worst-looking outer face of the shelves you've installed on the cubby assembly as the bottom piece. Lay the cubby assembly on its side with its bottom facing to the right and the back facing you. Take one of the bookshelf sides and align it on top of the cubby assembly, with the lower lines matching up to the shelf ends. The long point of the bevel should be underneath and pointing left. Drive the nails through the side piece and into the shelves of the cubby assembly.

20. Flip the assembly over. Start six nails in the other side piece on the face opposite the Xs. Align the side on top of the cubby assembly and drive in the nails.

21. Get the third shelf and choose its best side as the top. Slide it between the bookshelf sides, so that it covers the Xs on both sides, and nail it into place using three nails on each end.

each other about 6 inches apart, with their better sides facing out. Place the shelf that you started nails in on top of the cubby sides so that they cover the Xs. Align one cubby side precisely on the line for nailing, with the back of the cubby side flush with the back edge of the shelf. Drive the nails through the shelf and into the cubby side.

16. Align the other cubby side with the remaining layout line, with its back edge flush with the back edge of the shelf. Drive the nails through the shelf and into the cubby side. Make sure you've hit your mark with all the nails!

17. Turn over the assembly so that the other ends of the cubby sides point up. Start six nails in the other shelf, then nail it to the cubby sides. It should be much easier to align things this time. Remember to keep track of which is the front and which is the back!

Bookshelf Assembly

18. Bring the two bookshelf side pieces to your work surface. Start six nails in one of them on the face opposite the Xs, so that the bottom and middle layout lines each have three nails protruding slightly through them, next to the Xs. Each set

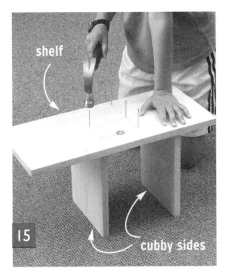
shelf

cubby sides

15

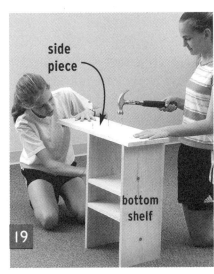
side piece

bottom shelf

19

top shelf

21

long roof piece

short roof piece

nailing together the roof pieces

23. Working with a partner, stand the shorter roof piece on its end and lay the longer piece on top of it, so that the end of the long piece is flush with the outer face of the short piece. Drive home the nails you just started. Handle this L-shaped section carefully to avoid flexing it and levering the joint apart.

24. Fit the ⅛-inch bit in the drill chuck. Stand the roof in an upright position, resting on the side pieces of the shelf assembly. The back edge of the roof must be flush with the back of the bookshelf, and the front will overhang. The layout lines will be visible on the underside of the bottom edges of the roof. On each side of the roof, drill two pilot holes about ½ inch below the layout lines and perpendicular to the plane of the roof, spacing them about 4 inches apart.

Raising the Roof

25. Keeping the bookshelf in an upright position, start a screw in one of the pilot holes on the roof pieces. Before the screw starts into the beveled edge of the bookshelf, your partner should make sure that the long point of the beveled side piece is on the layout line inside the attic (on the inside face of the roof).

26. While your partner holds the pieces tightly together, drive the screw in by hand with a screwdriver until the joint is

24

Roof Assembly

22. Bring the two roof pieces to your worktable. Take a look at the ends of the longer piece. On the end with the rougher cut, mark a series of Xs. Turn the board over and start three nails about ½ inch in from the end with the Xs. Your nails should be in a line across the board directly opposite the Xs on the other side.

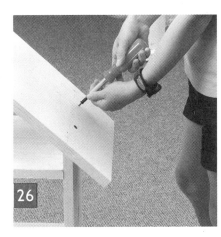

26

28

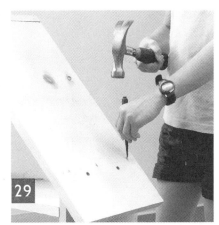

29

pulled tight. Then drive the other screw on the same side. If there is a gap in the joint, you may need to back the screw out, make sure the pieces are tight against each other, and then drive it in again.

27. Drive the two screws on the other side of the roof. Then set the Book House upright and admire your work!

28. Fit the 1/16-inch bit in the drill chuck. On one side of the roof, drill three holes vertically through the roof into the end of the bookshelf side. You should be able to dodge the screws by drilling one hole in the center and one hole in each outer edge. Remember that the roof has an overhang on the front, so the hole on that side will be farther in from the edge.

29. Drive ring-shank nails into each of the holes you drilled. Set the nails using a nail set, so that the heads of the nails are recessed below the surface of the roof. Remove the screws with a screwdriver.

31

30. Repeat the process on the other side of the roof: Drill three pilot holes, drive and set the ring-shank nails, then remove the screws.

31. Lay the Book House face-down. Use a framing square to check that the sides and shelves are square to each other and adjust them as needed. Then position on the frame the ply-wood back you cut earlier. Fasten the back to the frame with 1-inch panel nails, driving a nail every 6 inches or so around the perime-ter of the bookshelf and driving three or four nails into each shelf.

the bottom edge of the roof shingle was given the proper overhang first; now we're aligning the front of the shingle with the spacer

first roof shingle

spacer shingle

attaching the first shingle

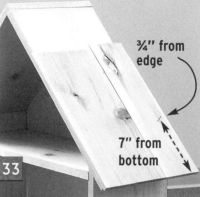

¾" from edge

7" from bottom

33

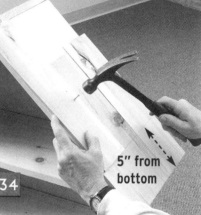

5" from bottom

34

Shingling the Roof

32. When we shingled our Book House, we hung the shingles a bit over the bottom and front edges of the roof to mimic the way shingles are applied on a real house. The easiest way to do this is to use the *butt* (the thick end) of an extra shingle as a spacer.

Start by placing a shingle on the front bottom edge of the roof, with its thicker end at the bottom. Hold the butt of the spacer against the bottom edge of the roof and set the bottom edge of the roof shingle flush with the edge of the spacer. Then move the spacer to the front edge of the roof and align the side of the

shingle with it. Now you can put the spacer down for a minute. Holding the roof shingle in place, drive two 1-inch panel nails through it and into the roof. The nails should be set about 7 inches up from the bottom end and ¾ inch in from each edge of the shingle.

33. Find a shingle that is wide enough to fill the rest of the roof space next to the first shingle and extend a bit past the back edge of the roof. Use your spacer to give it the proper overhang at the bottom edge of the roof and nail it in place. The portion of the shingle that overhangs on the back side of the Book House will be trimmed off later.

34. Start the second course of shingles by drawing a light pencil line 5 inches up from the bottom edge of the first course of shingles; this line marks the bottom of the second course. Select a shingle that is 1½ inches or so wider or narrower than the first shingle you put on (so that the joints between the lower shingles will be covered by the shingles above them). Align the bottom of your shingle on the pencil line, use your spacer to give it the proper overhang on the front of the roof, and nail it in place.

35. Find another one or two shingles to complete the roof's second course.

36

37

38

36. Apply the third and fourth courses of shingles. Drive the nails of the last course as close to the ridge as you can so that the nails will be covered by the ridge boards. Don't worry that the tops of the shingles will extend past the ridge of the roof, because they will be trimmed off later.

37. Using a handsaw, trim the tops of the shingles even with the ridge, using the slope of the roof on the opposite side as a guide for your saw blade.

38. Lay the Book House face-down. Saw the shingles on the back edge of the roof flush with

the back of the Book House, using it as a guide for your saw blade.

39. Repeat steps 32–38 — shingling four courses and trimming them at the ridge — on the other side of the roof.

40. To finish the roof, use panel nails to fasten on the two ridge boards. The first ridge board should be set with its top edge flush with the roof on the opposite side. The second ridge board should be set on the other side of the roof, with its top edge flush with the top edge of the first ridge board, as shown in the photo below.

Camille says: "Building the Book House wasn't the first time I had shingled. A few years ago I helped shingle part of our house. But it was a lot easier to shingle the Book House! For one thing, the Book House (unlike my real house) is a lot smaller than me.

"Shingling is like a game: You have to pick the right width of shingle so you don't get two courses with their joints lined up. Also you get to do one of my favorite parts of carpentry: hammering."

kids!

attaching the ridge boards

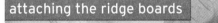

the edge of the second ridge board is flush with the face of the first

the ridge

The joints in each course are offset from the joints in the course below.

SHINGLING 101

A roof is always shingled from the bottom to the *ridge* (top). The first *course* (row) of shingles is nailed on along the *eaves* (the bottom edge of the roof), and other courses are nailed on above it. Each course overlaps the one below it, so that only about one third of the length of the shingles shows when you're finished. The nails used to fasten the shingles are covered by the shingles in the course above.

It's important to offset the joints in one course from the joints in the course below. That way, if water seeps through the joint or gap between the shingles, it runs into solid shingle below and doesn't leak through the roof. Finding a shingle just the right width to keep the joints offset is one of the fun challenges of shingling.

the eaves

Hanging the Door

41. Bring the door and the hinges to your work surface. Lay the door flat, with its back side facing up and its bottom facing you. Open the hinges, holding them so that the beveled side of the screw holes is visible on both *leaves* (the flat plates of a hinge).

42. Place one of the hinges on the right-hand edge of the door, about 1 inch down from the top, with its *barrel* (the cylinder in the middle of the hinge) hanging just past the edge of the door. Mark the position of the screw holes with a pencil. Remove the hinge and make starting holes with an awl or the tip of a finish nail. Put the hinge back in place and drive in the screws.

43. Repeat this process with the other hinge, positioning it about 1 inch up from the bottom, making sure that the hinge barrels are aligned so that the door will not bind.

44. Stand the door up on the shelf, to the left of the cubby, with its right-hand hinge leaves lying over the front edge of the cubby side. The hinge barrels should be centered between the door and the cubby side. Use a pencil to mark the centers of the screw holes. Use an awl or the tip of a finish nail to make starter holes *slightly above* the center marks you just made. Drive the hinge screws in place. When the screws are tightened, the bottom

of the door should lift just a bit off the shelf to keep it from rubbing when it opens and closes.

Painting and Decorating

45. The sky (or at least the roof, which doesn't need any kind of treatment, because shingles are best left just the way they are) is the limit when it comes to finishing your Book House. A simple coat of paint and contrasting trim will look great. But there are as many ways to decorate your Book House as there are ways to decorate real houses. Add a doorknob. Hang a painting. Have fun!

LEMONADE STAND

When we first built this project, our kids invited some of their friends over and we made two lemonade stands at the same time. It was hectic at moments, but it was great to have plenty of hands on deck when it came time to assemble the frames. The paint was barely dry when our first lemonade stand was set up on the sidewalk. It was a hot summery day and the young entrepreneurs sold a lot of lemonade, shaded by the awning they'd made for themselves. For the rest of the week, the lemonade stand moved from one friend's house to another.

Making a lemonade stand will take your family many hours. It will probably be challenging, maybe even difficult at times, but you will get to learn and practice many new carpentry tricks. Altogether it is a very satisfying project. It begins with measuring, cutting, drilling, and nailing and ends with return on investment and marketing savvy — not to mention a nice cold drink.

What You'll Need

TOOLS

Handsaw or jigsaw

Drill

1¼-inch Forstner bit

¼-inch drill bit

⅛-inch drill bit

Phillips-head screwdriver

Hammer

Framing square

Awl

Combination square or Speed Square

Utility knife

Staple gun

Clamps

Pencil

Measuring tape

Safety glasses

MATERIALS

One 4-foot by 8-foot sheet of ¼-inch luaun or birch plywood

Six 10-foot lengths of 1x4

One 10-foot length of 1x10

Four 7-foot lengths of 1¹⁄₁₆-inch closet pole

One 16-inch length of ¼-inch dowel

One sheet of sandpaper

Colorful cloth for the awning (approximately 42 inches x 76 inches)

Colorful cloth for the pennants

Cloth ribbon (optional)

Colorful paint

Paintbrushes

FASTENERS

One pound 1¼-inch drywall screws

One pound 2-inch drywall screws

Two pounds 4d galvanized box nails

⁵⁄₁₆-inch staples

Carpenter's wood glue

Fabric glue

Forstner bit

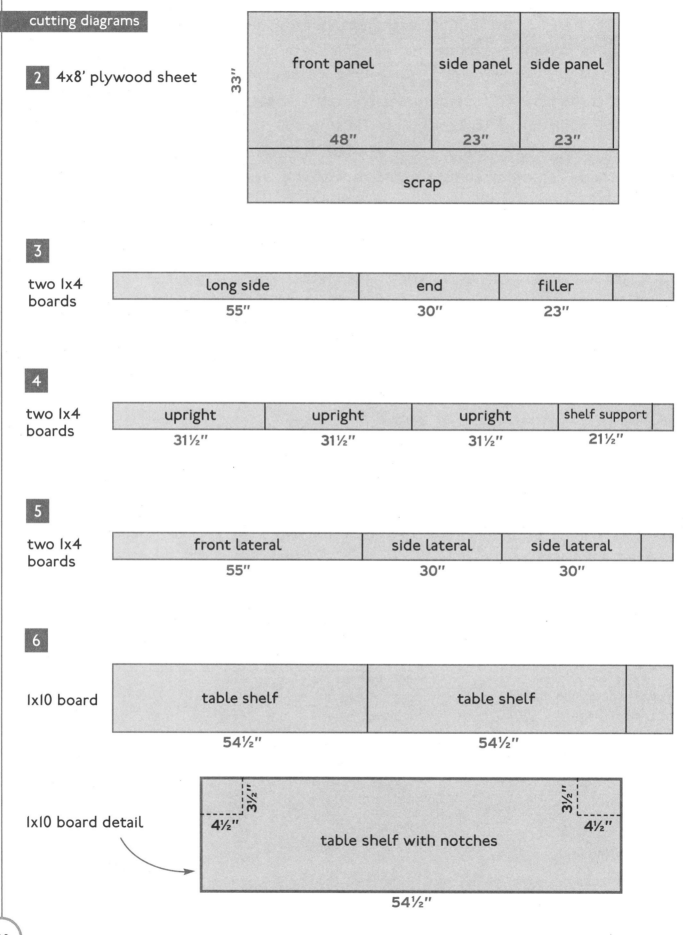

2 4x8' plywood sheet

33"

| front panel | side panel | side panel |
| 48" | 23" | 23" |

scrap

3

two 1x4 boards

| long side | end | filler |
| 55" | 30" | 23" |

4

two 1x4 boards

| upright | upright | upright | shelf support |
| 31½" | 31½" | 31½" | 21½" |

5

two 1x4 boards

| front lateral | side lateral | side lateral |
| 55" | 30" | 30" |

6

1x10 board

| table shelf | table shelf |
| 54½" | 54½" |

1x10 board detail

3½"
4½"
3½"
4½"

table shelf with notches

54½"

Getting Started:
Layout and Cutting

1. You're going to start by cutting all the wood to size, so set up a comfortable cutting station. You'll need a sturdy work surface (such as a table or a pair of sawhorses), a handsaw and/or a jigsaw (and an electrical outlet nearby so you can plug it in), clamps, a pencil, a measuring tape, a combination square or Speed Square, and safety glasses.

2. Measure and rip the sheet of plywood so that it measures 33 inches by 96 inches. Crosscut this piece into the front panel, measuring 48 inches by 33 inches, and two side panels, each measuring 23 inches by 33 inches. Keep these pieces together as a set and put them aside for now.

3. Next you'll cut the lengths for the awning roof frame. Stack two of the 10-foot lengths of 1x4 boards with their ends even. Cut two 55-inch pieces; these will become the long sides. Cut another pair 30 inches long; these will become the ends of the frame. Finally, cut two 23-inch lengths; these will be the filler pieces. Keep these parts together as a set and put them aside.

4. Stack two more 10-foot lengths of 1x4 board. Cut three pairs (six pieces) 31½ inches long. These are the uprights. Now cut two more pieces at 21½ inches. These will be the shelf supports.

Keep these pieces together as a set and put them aside.

5. Stack the two remaining 10-foot lengths of 1x4 board. Cut one pair (two pieces) at 55 inches for the front laterals and two pairs (four pieces) at 30 inches for the side laterals. Keep these pieces together as a set and put them aside.

6. Cut the 1x10 board into two 54½-inch lengths. These will be the shelves inside the lemonade stand. One of the boards needs to be notched to fit correctly. Lay out a notch at each end of one of the pieces, as shown on the facing page. The notches measure 4½ inches along the length of the piece and 3½ inches along its width. Using a handsaw or jigsaw, cut out the notches. Keep the two pieces together as a set and put them aside.

crosscutting stacked boards

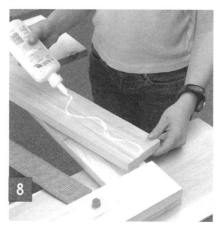

Awning Assembly

7. Now it's time to transform your worktable into an assembly station. Bring the pieces of the awning roof frame to the table. Place the 30-inch end pieces parallel to each other on the table. Lay the 55-inch side pieces perpendicular to the 30-inch pieces, with their ends resting on top of the ends of the 30-inch

pieces, so that the pieces form a rectangle. Set the 23-inch filler pieces on top of the 30-inch end pieces, between the ends of the 55-inch side pieces. You should now have a rectangle in one plane on the top. Square up the pieces using a framing square along the outer edges.

8. Carefully lift up the filler pieces and put wood glue along

their bottom surfaces. Replace them and recheck the alignment with a framing square. Drive three 1¼-inch screws through each filler into the end piece below to fasten the two pieces together. (These screws will be covered later by the awning fabric, so if the pieces slip out of alignment while you're drilling, just remove the screw, realign the parts, and drive in the screw at a new location close by.)

9. Lift up one of the 55-inch side pieces and put wood glue on the top surfaces of the two ends beneath it. Replace the side piece. Holding the side in place, drive a 1¼-inch screw through each end, into the end piece beneath. These screws will serve to clamp the pieces together while the glue sets and will be removed later. Repeat the process with the other side piece.

10. Now check the alignment one last time and try to get the frame as close to square as you can. (Perfection is not required.) Then set the awning roof frame aside.

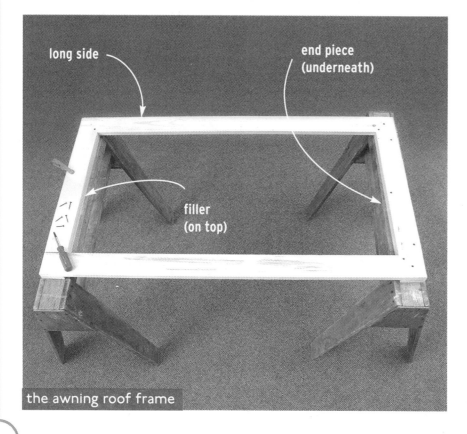

long side

end piece (underneath)

filler (on top)

the awning roof frame

Keep the drill straight!

Drilling

11. You're now going to drill holes in all the laterals and in the four corners of the awning roof frame. Bring all the lateral pieces to the table. Mark the center of both ends of all the pieces by measuring 1¾ inches in from the end and 1¾ inches in from either side. Then use an awl to punch a small hole into the center marks.

12. Put the Forstner bit in the drill chuck. Place one of the marked lateral pieces on top of a piece of scrap wood and clamp it down. Running the drill at a slow speed, drill all the way through the piece at the center mark at each end. Repeat at both ends for all the pieces. When you are finished, you should have two 55-inch front pieces and four 30-inch side pieces with holes drilled through at both ends.

13. Bring to the table the awning roof frame you worked on before. Remove the center screws holding the corner joints together. Turn the frame over and lay out holes centered on

each corner, 1¾ inches in from either side of the corner. Punch the center of each hole with an awl, then use the Forstner bit to drill a hole all the way through both pieces of each frame corner.

The Awning Roof

14. Position the awning roof frame so that the filler pieces face up. Bring the awning cloth to the table. Position one of the longer edges of the fabric so that it is centered lengthwise on one long side of the frame. Fold about

1½ inches of the fabric over the long side and staple it along the back edge of the frame.

15. Fold the cloth back off the frame and spread some fabric glue along the top surface of the frame. Apply a circle of glue around each of the holes; this will help prevent the fabric from fraying when it is cut out from over these holes later. Lay the cloth back into position and staple it around the rest of the perimeter, pulling it taut as you go. For a polished look, glue cloth ribbon over the staples.

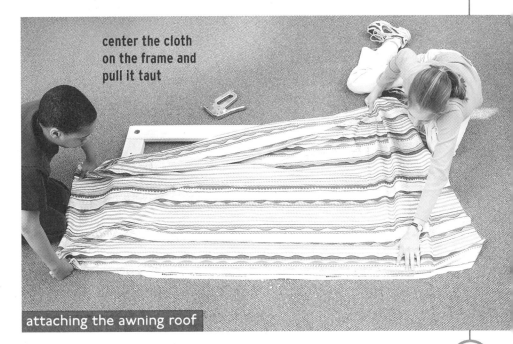

center the cloth on the frame and pull it taut

attaching the awning roof

When someone else
is nailing nearby,
watch your fingers!

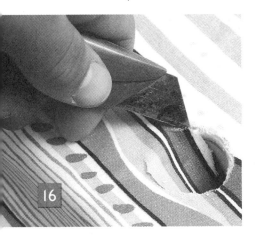

16

16. After the glue has thoroughly dried, use a utility knife to cut the fabric out of the holes you drilled in the frame.

The Framework

17. Gather the laterals, the uprights, the shelf supports, and the plywood panels. Clear off your assembly station and set up the drill with a ⅛-inch drill bit. Also grab the Phillips-head screwdriver and the 2-inch drywall screws.

18. Lay the two 55-inch front laterals flat on the table. Square a line 3½ inches in from each end of both laterals. These lines mark the position of the outer edges of the uprights. Then set the laterals on edge, parallel to each other, with the layout lines facing each other.

19. Set the 31½-inch uprights between — perpendicular to — the laterals, positioning their outer edges just inside the layout lines. This is a good time to use a clamp or to get a helper to hold pieces in alignment. At each joint

where a lateral meets an upright, predrill two holes through the lateral into the end of the upright, then drive a 2-inch drywall screw into each hole. You have now successfully built the front frame!

20. Assemble the side frames the same way, using the 30-inch laterals and the 31½-inch uprights.

21. Choose one end of each side frame assembly to be the bottom of the frame. Hook your tape measure on the bottom of the frame, measure up 27 inches, and square a line at that point across the inside of the upright. This line marks where the top edge of a shelf support will go. Repeat for each upright on each frame, for a total of four lines.

Camille says: "There are many hard parts to building the Lemonade Stand, so in comparison, hammering on the plywood was easy. It's funny that when I work on projects with other people, my dad tells them the same thing he used to tell me: Let the hammer do the work! Once you get it, hammering is one of the most fun parts of carpentry."

kids!

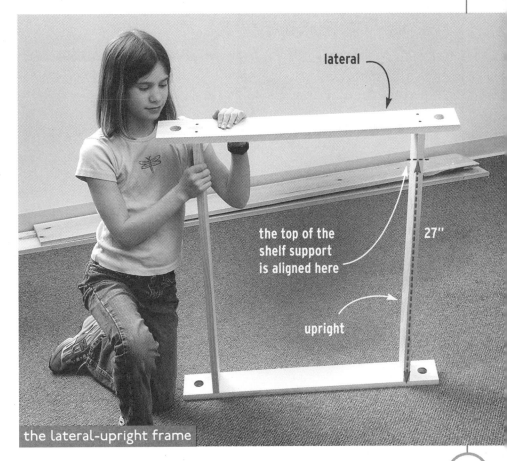

lateral

the top of the shelf support is aligned here

27"

upright

the lateral-upright frame

23

upright

lateral

shelf support

27"

attaching the shelf support

AVOIDING BOUNCE

When you're nailing the plywood to the frame, keep the part you're hammering on close to the sawhorse or table. If you don't, the plywood will bounce around and make it hard to drive the nails. Also, take a look at the underside of the frame as you're nailing. If you don't nail straight in, the nail tip will start to poke out from the frame. If that happens, you should pull out the nail and start a new one nearby. And it's a lot easier to pull out a nail before it's driven in all the way!

22. Align a 21½-inch shelf support between the uprights in each frame, with its top edge just below the lines you marked. Using the ⅛-inch drill bit, drill two pilot holes through the uprights into each end of the shelf supports. Then drive a 2-inch drywall screw (eight screws total) through each hole to fasten the pieces in place.

Applying the Plywood

23. Match each of the three pieces of plywood to a frame. The grain of the plywood should run horizontally. Working one at a time, lay the frames flat on your work surface, with the plywood panels aligned on top of them. Drive box nails through the plywood into the frame every 6 to 8 inches around the perimeter. Locate the shelf supports on the side frames and drive a couple of box nails through the plywood into them for added strength.

24. When you're done fastening the plywood, check over all your frames for protruding nails. If you find one, pull it out and drive in another in a new spot nearby.

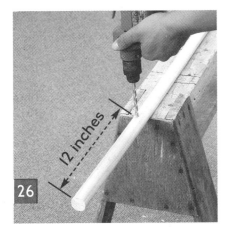

26

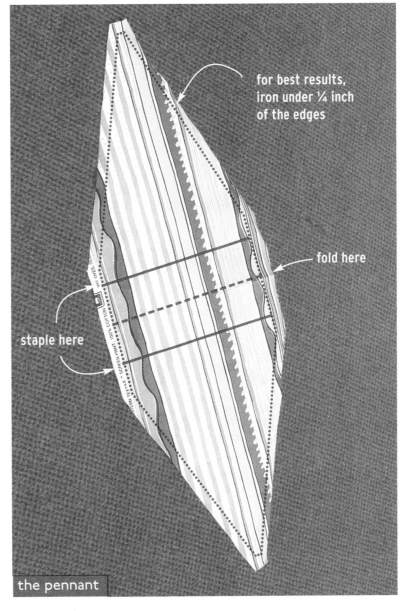

for best results,
iron under ¼ inch
of the edges

fold here

staple here

the pennant

Flags Up!

25. Verify that each length of closet pole is exactly 7 feet in length. If it's not, cut it to size.

26. Put the ¼-inch bit in the drill chuck. Measure and mark a point 12 inches in from one end of each flagstaff. At that mark, drill a hole all the way through the flagstaff. At assembly time, a dowel pin slipped through this hole will hold up the awning roof.

27. Cut four 3-inch lengths of the ¼-inch dowel to serve as pins. Round the ends by rubbing them on sandpaper. This is a good task for the youngest member of the work crew.

28. Cut two pieces of pennant cloth as shown in the diagram (above right). Fold over each cloth along the dotted line as shown, and staple the two layers together along the solid line. You now have created a sleeve for the flagstaff to fit into. Sew or staple the top of each sleeve so that it will stay in place on the flagstaff.

A Painting Party

29. Painting and decorating the Lemonade Stand should be a fun and relaxed activity. Bright colors will attract more customers, and don't shy away from bold designs. Take apart the stand so that you can work on each section separately. Count on using two coats of paint, and let the paint dry between coats. Leaving the flagstaffs bare is the most practical course, because paint can make the flagstaffs stick during assembly. There's no need to paint the inside of the Lemonade Stand because the public will not see it.

When you buy the paint, find out whether the store carries blackboard paint. Once you've applied a few coats of blackboard paint to a surface, you have a perfect place to write your menu and prices. You might even consider painting the front panel of the stand with blackboard paint.

Setting It Up!

The Lemonade Stand is designed so that setting it up and taking it down will be manageable for two or three capable children. It may take a little practice. Proceeding in the right order will help!

1. Arrange the three panels in a horseshoe shape with their ends overlapping and the flagstaff holes aligned. The ends of the center panel should rest on top of the ends of the side panels.

2. Have one or two people hold the front corners of the stand steady while another person spreads the ends of the two sides apart and slips the two tabletop shelves in place. Put the notched shelf in first, with the notches facing toward the front of the lemonade stand. The notches will fit around the corner joint and allow the shelf to fit snugly against the plywood. Then pull the two sides back into place in the horsehoe shape.

3. Lay the awning roof flat on top of the stand. Align the four holes in the awning roof with the four holes on the top of the stand. Lift the flagstaffs high and slide them down through the awning roof holes, through the holes in the top of the stand, and through the matching holes at the bottom of the stand. Here is where your careful drilling will pay off. It may take a little jostling and adjusting to get the poles to go down through, but you'll quickly get the hang of it.

align the holes in the corners

set the notched shelf in first

the ends of the front panel rest on top of the ends of the side panels

4. Have two of your tallest crew members lift the awning roof up high. The trick here is to keep the roof level as it goes up and not let it bind up and pull the flagstaffs out of their holes. If you're having trouble with one or more of the flagstaffs, have an extra person turn that flagstaff, spinning it in its hole, as the roof goes up. (This should be a chaotic, laughter-filled moment.) Keep lifting until the roof frame goes past the holes you drilled in the flagstaffs for the dowel pins. Then insert the pins in the hole.

5. Settle the roof frame on top of the dowel pins. Slip the pennants onto the tops of flagstaffs. Bring out your lemonade, set up some chairs, and you are ready for business!

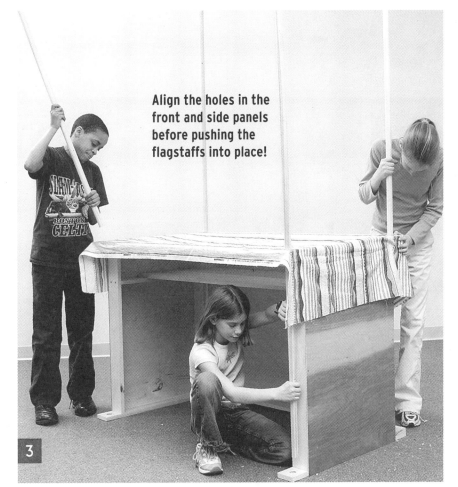

Align the holes in the front and side panels before pushing the flagstaffs into place!

3

4

puppet theater

A good puppet theater is an invitation to play. Climb in, crouch down, and put on a show. Your audience can see your puppets but they can't see you!

The Puppet Theater is actually the Lemonade Stand (page 114) with a different roof. Like the Lemonade Stand, it is a complex project and can take a few days of hard work to finish. You'll need to decide what color to paint it, what cloth you'd like for the curtain and the ruffle, and whether or not you want some fancy gold embellishments here and there. Once you're done, you'll have a theater made to your every specification. Let the show begin!

What You'll Need

TOOLS

Handsaw or jigsaw

Tubing cutter or hacksaw

Drill

1¼-inch Forstner bit

⁵⁄₁₆-inch drill bit

⅛-inch drill bit

Screw gun or Phillips-head screwdriver

Framing square

Clamps

Staple gun

⁵⁄₁₆-inch staples

Scissors

Pencil

Safety glasses

Clothes iron

MATERIALS

Two 10-foot lengths of 1x6

Two 6-foot lengths of ¼-inch copper refrigeration tubing

11 feet of colorful cloth (width no less than 42 inches) for the curtains

11 feet of colorful cloth for the ruffle

15 feet of colorful ribbon for seaming the ruffle

24 curtain loops with clips

Materials for building the Lemonade Stand bottom (if you haven't built it already; see page 115)

FASTENERS

One pound 1¼-inch drywall screws

Four 1-inch #12 sheet-metal screws

Carpenter's wood glue

Fabric glue

to parents

The plans for the Puppet Theater are identical to those for the Lemonade Stand except that for this project you will not need to make shelves and you will build a curtain-top roof instead of an awning roof. If you build one of each kind of top, you will have all the pieces for lemonade sales by day and dramatic performances by night.

If your kids are interested only in the Puppet Theater, you'll need to start by working with the Lemonade Stand instructions and then switch to the theater instructions when you're ready to build the curtain top. If this is your plan, be sure to read through both projects ahead of time so you don't get confused along the way!

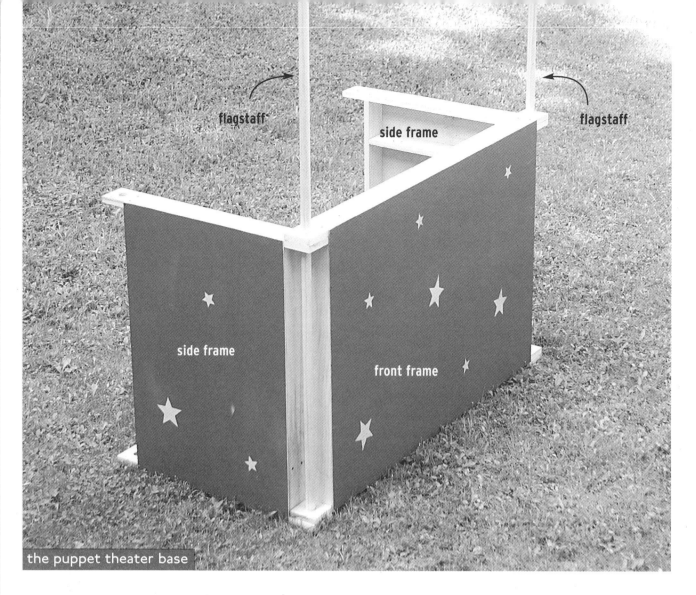

flagstaff

side frame

flagstaff

side frame

front frame

the puppet theater base

Setting the Stage

1. If you've built the Lemonade Stand, you already have most of what you need for this project. If you haven't built the Lemonade Stand, turn back to page 114 and get started. You'll need to build the three bottom panels and cut the flagstaffs to size. Don't make the shelves, though — they'll only get in the puppeteers' way!

Constructing the Curtain-Top Frame

2. Stack the two 1x6 boards with their ends even. Cut two pieces 59 inches long; these will become the long sides of the curtain-top frame. Cut another pair 34 inches long; these pieces will become the short sides of the frame. Finally, cut two 23-inch lengths; these will become the filler pieces.

3. Place the 34-inch side pieces to your left and right on your work surface. Set the 59-inch front and back pieces perpendicular to the 34-inch side pieces, with their ends resting on top of the ends of the 34-inch pieces, to form a rectangle. Set the 23-inch filler pieces on top of the 34-inch end pieces, between the ends of the 59-inch front and back pieces. You should now have a rectangle in one plane on

two 1x6 boards	59"	34"	23"	
	long side	short side	filler piece	

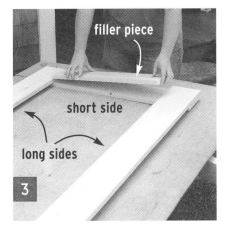

filler piece

short side

long sides

3

4

5

the top. Square up the pieces using a framing square along the outer edges.

4. Carefully lift up the filler pieces and put carpenter's glue along their bottom surfaces. Replace them and recheck the alignment with a framing square. Drive four 1¼-inch screws through each filler piece into the end piece below to fasten the two pieces together.

5. Lift up one of the long sides and put glue on the top surfaces of the two ends beneath it. Replace the piece. Holding the long side in place, drive three 1¼-inch screws through each end, into the side piece below. Avoid driving a screw in the extreme outside corner of each corner; you'll be drilling holes for the curtain rods there later.

6. Repeat step 5 with the other long side.

7. Check the alignment one last time and try to get the frame as close to square as you can. (Perfection is not required.)

note that there are no screws in the extreme outside corners

the finished curtain-top frame

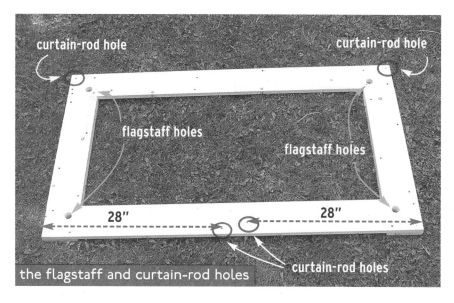

curtain-rod hole   curtain-rod hole

flagstaff holes

flagstaff holes

28"   28"

the flagstaff and curtain-rod holes

curtain-rod holes

point where the two lines intersect. Do the same on the other far corner. If there is a screw in the way at these crosshairs, take it out now.

12. Put the ⁵⁄₁₆-inch bit in the drill chuck. Drill a hole all the way through the frame at each of the four points you've marked. These smaller holes are for the curtain-rod ends.

Making the Awning Ruffle

13. Cut your ruffle cloth into three 12-inch-wide strips. (Each one will measure 11 feet by 12 inches.) Fold each piece in half lengthwise and run a hot iron along the folds. You should now have three 11-foot by 6-inch lengths of cloth.

14. Turn the curtain-top frame so that the filler pieces face up and one of the long sides hangs about 2 inches off the front of your work surface. Clamp the frame in place. Then find the center of the front edge of the frame and make a small pencil mark there.

Drilling

8. When the glue is dry, turn the frame over. At each corner, square a line 3¾ inches in from each outside edge, so that you have two lines that intersect. Use an awl to punch each intersection point.

9. Put the 1¼-inch Forstner bit in the drill chuck. Set the spur of the bit in one of the small holes you punched with the awl. Drill a hole all the way through the long side and the end piece beneath it. Repeat at the other three corners.

10. Turn the curtain top frame upside down on your work surfaces, with the filler pieces facing down and the short sides to your left and right. Square lines across the nearer long side 28 inches in from either end. On one of these lines, mark a point 1 inch in from the near edge of the frame. On the other line, mark a point 2 inches in from the near edge of the frame.

11. Reach across to the long side away from you and square a line 1 inch in from each edge at one of the far corners. Mark the

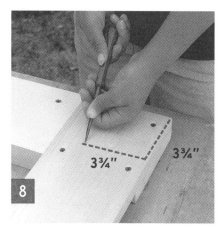

3¾"   3¾"

8

9

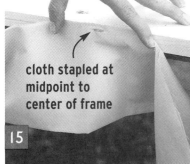

cloth stapled at midpoint to center of frame

15

Keep the pleats flush with the top edge of the frame.

17

15. Find the midpoint of one of the pieces of ruffle cloth. At the midpoint, staple the unfolded edge of the cloth to the center of the front edge of the frame, keeping the edge of the cloth flush with the top edge of the frame. Take a look: The unfolded edge of cloth should be stapled to the wood and the folded edge should hang down.

16. Grab hold of the top edge of the cloth a few inches to the left of the midpoint. Bring that top edge back against the midpoint staple, making a loop of cloth that points out toward you. Keeping the top edge in position, flatten the loop to the left and staple its end to the edge of the frame. The new staple should be just about an inch away from the midpoint staple. You've just made one pleat!

17. To make the next one, grab the cloth a few inches to the left of the pleat, pull the top edge back to the staple you just placed, fold the loop of cloth down to the left, and staple it flush to the top edge of the frame.

Working to the left, create a series of flat, folded pleats across the top of your theater, like those at the tops of old-fashioned curtains. Try to make your folds even, stapling every inch or so. (Pleating may be an easier task with two people working together, one to fold and hold the cloth and the other to staple.)

18. When you reach the end of the cloth, staple the end to the frame, get another length of fabric, and keep going. Overlap the new fabric over the "ruffle" of the old fabric by an inch or so. When you get to the corner of your frame, turn and reclamp the frame on the work surface and turn the corner with your fabric.

19. Continue pleating until you reach the end of the short side. There, cut the fabric about ½ inch longer than you need and fold this extra underneath before you put the last staple in just before the corner.

18

the finished ruffle

20. Go back to the middle of the front and repeat the pleating and stapling process, working to the right, until you have completed the ruffle all the way across the front and the other short side.

21. Glue a long piece of ribbon along the top of the ruffle to hide the staples, starting at the end of one short side, moving across the front, and finishing on the other short side. Cut off the excess ribbon when you are finished. Gluing, smoothing, and holding the ribbon in place may require a few extra sets of hands. The result will be a beautiful finished ruffle.

21

Crafting Curtains

22. Cut the curtain fabric in half. Each piece should be 5½ feet long (but longer is okay).

23. Lay one of the pieces of fabric flat on your work surface. On one of the long sides, fold over 1 inch of the edge, iron it down, and staple it in place. Repeat this process on both short sides. Then bring the other piece of fabric to your work surface and iron and staple the same three folds.

24. Now you're ready to fold, iron, and staple the remaining long sides. Figure out how much you'll have to fold over to make the final width of each cloth 36 inches. If your fold is more than 2 inches, use two or even three rows of staples to hold it down. Or you can trim off some of the extra cloth to make your fold less than 2 inches.

25. Clip the curtain loops to one of the long sides of each piece, starting at a corner and placing a clip every 6 inches or so.

to parents

In our directions we have advised stapling cloth only because this is not a sewing book and we do not want new carpenters to have to learn too many new skills at once. However, any stapling of cloth that we have advised can be replaced by sewing, if you prefer. Also, there are many cloth-gluing products available that work well; they're another option to consider.

place the clips about every 6 inches

the ready-to-hang curtain

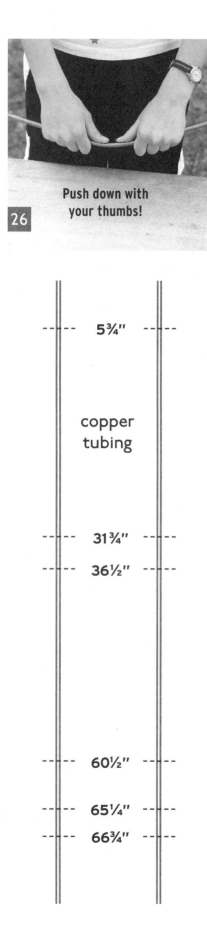

Push down with your thumbs!

26

5¾"

copper
tubing

31¾"

36½"

60½"

65¼"

66¾"

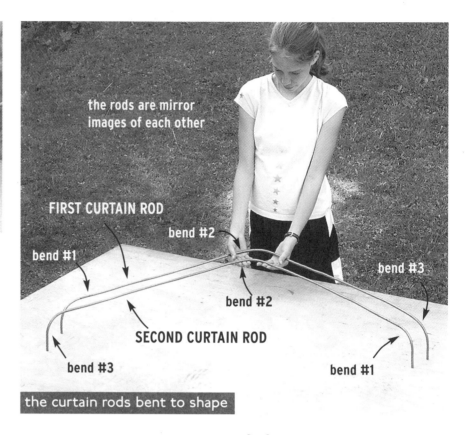

the rods are mirror images of each other

FIRST CURTAIN ROD

bend #2

bend #1

bend #2

bend #3

SECOND CURTAIN ROD

bend #3

bend #1

the curtain rods bent to shape

Shaping the Curtain Rods

26. Uncoil the two lengths of copper tubing, bending them until they are basically straight. To bend (or straighten) the tubing, grasp it with both hands, with your thumbs pointing toward each other and about an inch apart. Gently push in with your thumbs until you feel the tubing move. Shift your hands along the tubing and press down again with your thumbs, bending the tubing just a little in each place along its length to avoid creating kinks.

27. When the copper tubing is straightened, lay the two lengths side by side and mark them together at 5¾, 31¾, 36½, 60½, 65¼, and 66¾ inches from one end.

28. Grab a length of tubing in both hands, with the end you measured from in your right hand. About 1½ inches from the end, begin bending the tubing. Bend a little, move your hands farther down, and bend a little more. When you reach the first layout mark on the tubing, stop bending and check your progress. Your goal is to make the tubing turn 90 degrees evenly between the end of the tube and the first layout mark. Adjust your curve by bending more (or unbending if necessary), spreading your efforts along the whole length of bent tubing. (Perfection is not required, and you will be able to make adjustments later.)

29. Grip the tube at the second mark (31¾ inches from the end), with the bent end on your right and pointing up. Begin making a second bend along a horizontal plane, trying to complete a 90-degree turn by the time you reach the third layout mark. You should end up with a left-hand bend.

30. Hold the tubing with the unworked end on your left, the second bend pointing downward, and the first bend pointing toward you. Position your thumbs at the fourth layout mark and begin bending along a horizontal plane, trying to complete a 90-degree turn as you reach the fifth layout mark. Use a tubing cutter or a hacksaw to cut the piece at the last mark.

31. The second curtain rod will be a mirror image of the first. Repeat step 26 to make the first bend. To make the second bend, hold the tubing with its curved end to the left of your hands and pointing up, and move your hands to the right as you bend. For the final bend, hold the rod so that the second bend is to the left of your hands and points downward, and move your hands to the right as you bend. Cut the piece at the final layout mark.

32. Place the curtain frame upside down with the ⁵⁄₁₆-inch holes in the corners closest to you. Hold the completed curtain rods up to the curtain frame to check their alignment, remembering that they overlap at the center of the frame. Insert the ends a short way into the ⁵⁄₁₆-inch

aligning the curtain rods

holes until the rods support themselves. The rods should curve around the outside of the larger holes (so that on opening night the curtain can follow the same path around the pole that will run through the holes). If your rods are out of alignment, bend them into position now.

33. Remove the curtain rods one at a time and slip the curtains onto them. Insert the ends of the rods back into the ⁵⁄₁₆-inch holes. Work the ends of the rods down into the holes until they reach all the way through the frame to the work surface.

34. Set the frame on edge with its top surface facing you. Drive the #12 sheet-metal screws into the tubing until the screw head contacts the wood frame. This is

an unorthodox use of screws and copper tubing, but with some extra force, the threads should bite into the copper and flare it tight against the sides of the drilled hole.

35. Assemble your puppet theater using the directions for the Lemonade Stand (pages 124–125). Grab your puppets and put on a show!

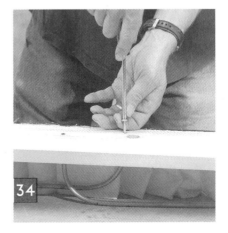
34

index

Page numbers in *italics* indicate illustrations and photographs.

A

Adding measurements, 36
Allegra's Table, *92*, 92-101
Angled cut, *14*, 14-15
Apron, for Drawing Table, *96*, *96*, 98, *98*
Arrow String Art, 45, *45*
Awning roof, for Lemonade Stand 118-19, *118-19*, 124-25, *125*

B

Bevel cut, 14-15, *14-15*, 58, *58*
Birdhouses, *46*, 46-55, *52*
Bits for drilling, 20, *20*, 23
Blade binding, 12
Block plane, 26-29, *26-29*
Book House, *102*, 102-13
Bounce when hammering, 122, *122*
Brace and bit, *20*, 22, *22*
Buttons, 99, *99*

C

Cage, Cricket, *62*, 62-67, *67*
Checkerboard, 34-37, *34-37*
Circles, compass for, 41, *41*
Clamps, 94, *94*, 98, *98*
Combination square, *30*, 31
Compass for circles, 41, *41*
Compound cut, 14, *14*
Countersink drill bit, 20, *20*
Cricket Cage, *62*, 62-67, *67*
Crosscut saws, 10, *10*
Crosscutting, 14, *14*
Crosshairs, marking, 21, *21*
Curl, Perfect, 28-29, *28-29*
Curtain rods, shaping, 134-35, *134-35*
Curtain top, for Puppet Theater 128-30, *128-30*, 130-32, *130-32*, 133-35, *133-35*

D

Direct measurement, 32
Dividing, equal, *33*, 33-34
Double-Bridge String Art, 43, *43*, 45, *45*
Dowels, cutting, 64, 65, 66
Drilling, 20-25, *20-25*, 88
Drywall screws, 23, *23*

F

Finish coat, 101
Flags, 123, *123*, 125, *125*
Flat-head screwdriver, *23*
Flip It, *82*, 82-91, *91*
Forstner drill bit, 20, *20*
Framing square, *30*, 31, 36-37, *36-37*
Furniture Factory, 16-19, *16-19*

G

Gluing, 95, *95*, 99, *99*, 100

H

Hammering, 6-9, *6-9*, 18, *18*, 122, *122*
Hand drill, 20-22, 20-23
Handsaw, 10-12, *10-12*, 15
Hinges, 113, *113*
Horse Sawhorses, *74*, 74-81
House, Book, *102*, 102-13

I

Iron, adjusting on a block plane, 27

J

Jigsaw, *10*, 13, *13*, 15

K

Kerf, *10*, 11
Kids' building workshop, 1-3

L

Lemonade Stand, *114*, 114-25

M

Mane for sawhorses, 81, *81*
Math and measuring, 32, 36
Measuring, 30-37, *30-37*
Momentum, when hammering, 6-8, *7-8*

N

Nail set, *6*, 9, *9*

P

Painting, 51, 55, 61, 67, 73, 81, 113, 123
Paper rule, 33, *33*
Pennants, 123, *123*
Perch for birdhouse, 51, *51*
Perfect Curl, 28-29, *28-29*
Perfect Toolbox, *68*, 68-73
Phillips-head screwdriver, *23*
Planing, 26-29, *26-29*
Pleating ruffle, *131*, 131-32
Plugs, 99, *99*
Polyurethane varnish, 93, 101

**Power drills, *20-21*, 20-23
Predrilling, 23, *23*
Pulling out a nail, 8-9, *9*
Pull saw, 10-12, *10-12*, 14
Puppet Theater, *126*, 126-35
Push saw, *10*, 10-12

R

Ripping, 14, *14*
Ruffle, awning, 130-32, *130-32*
Ruler, 30, *30*, *32-33*, 33, 35, *35*

S

Safety, 2
Sanding, 89, *89*, 100, *100*
Sawhorses, *74*, 74-81
Sawing, 10-19, *10-19*
Screws, 23, *23*
Shelves, 104, *105-7*, 107
Shingling, 110-12, *110-12*
Single Birdhouse, *52*, 52-55
Spacers, 100, *101*
Speed Square, 15, *30-31*, 31, 32
Square cut, 58-59, *58-59*
Squares, *30-32*, 31
Squaring a line, 32, *32*
Stand, Lemonade, *114*, 114-25
Stapling, *131*, 131-32, 133
Stenciling footprints, 61, *61*
Stool, Sturdy, *56*, 56-61, *61*
String Art, 40-46, *40-46*
Sturdy Stool, *56*, 56-61, *61*
Sunset String Art, 44, *44*
Sunshine String Art, 44, *44*

T

Table, Allegra's, *92*, 92-101
Tail for sawhorses, 81, *81*
Theater, Puppet, *126*, 126-35
Toolbox, Perfect, *68*, 68-73
Tools, 3
Twin Birdhouse, *46*, 46-51
"Twist" drill bit, 20, *20*

U

Utility knives, 84

W

Wood plugs and buttons, 99, *99*

Y

You Name It, 24-25, *24-25*